ALSO BY GEORGE PACKER

NONFICTION

*Our Man: Richard Holbrooke
and the End of the American Century*

The Unwinding: An Inner History of the New America

Interesting Times: Writings from a Turbulent Decade

The Assassins' Gate: America in Iraq

Blood of the Liberals

The Village of Waiting

FICTION

Central Square

The Half Man

PLAYS

Betrayed

AS EDITOR

All Art Is Propaganda: Critical Essays by George Orwell

Facing Unpleasant Facts: Narrative Essays by George Orwell

*The Fight Is for Democracy:
Winning the War of Ideas in America and the World*

LAST
BEST HOPE

LAST BEST HOPE

AMERICA IN CRISIS AND RENEWAL

GEORGE PACKER

FARRAR, STRAUS AND GIROUX
NEW YORK

Farrar, Straus and Giroux
120 Broadway, New York 10271

Portions of this work originally appeared in *The Atlantic* and *The New Yorker*.

Library of Congress Control Number: 2021934375
ISBN: 978-0-374-60366-3

Designed by Gretchen Achilles

Our books may be purchased in bulk for promotional, educational,
or business use. Please contact your local bookseller or the Macmillan Corporate
and Premium Sales Department at 1-800-221-7945, extension 5442,
or by email at MacmillanSpecialMarkets@macmillan.com.

www.fsgbooks.com
www.twitter.com/fsgbooks • www.facebook.com/fsgbooks

1   3   5   7   9   10   8   6   4   2

For Charlie and Julia

and their grandparents

Nancy, Bob, and Marie

I speak the password primeval, I give the sign of
   democracy,
By God! I will accept nothing which all cannot have
   their counterpart of on the same terms.

—WALT WHITMAN

CONTENTS

LAST
BEST HOPE

am an American. No, I don't want pity. In the long story of our experiment in self-government, the world's pity has taken the place of admiration, hostility, awe, envy, fear, affection, and repulsion. Pity is more painful than any of these, and after pity comes indifference, which would be intolerable.

I know a woman who said of her own husband and children, "They're not the people I'd choose to be quarantined with." Are my fellow citizens the people I'd choose to be quarantined with? Well, there's no choice. They're mine, and I'm theirs. During the time of separation we Americans, with our dollars and easy smiles and loud voices, have not been welcome abroad. U.S. passports, once worth stealing, are no good. Formerly mobile, we've been trapped with ourselves and one another. A lot of Americans have explored their options for expatriation—a deceased Irish grandfather, a suddenly promising Canadian girlfriend, an open invitation from the government of Ghana, a loophole in New

Zealand's citizenship law. As for me, I'm staying put, and not just because these exit strategies are not available to me. I want to see how it all turns out—for my children if not myself. Whether a huge multi-everything democracy can survive or will perish from the earth is a matter of interest, and not only for us.

The virus gave us this one gift: it interrupted us. The mask wearing, the grocery wiping, the regretted handshake, the risk in this muffled person headed my way on the sidewalk: it became impossible to pass through the world in the normal bovine manner. The virus forced us to look at ourselves and for once pay the kind of attention that we've always taken for granted from others.

I don't mean the image-check of a teenager glancing at a smartphone screen or store window. This attention is a long middle-aged stare in the mirror at a face rising from a dark background. It's not the face I expect to see. Vertical etchings under the cheekbones, the color of exhaustion around the eyes, what's left of the hair badly in need of professional organizing. Instead of the calm wisdom expected by now, there's an expression of uncertainty, a hint of muted panic. The stare brings a shock of estrangement. Don't look too long or I'll stop knowing who this is.

The time of separation made us strangers not just to one another but also to ourselves. A young girl told her parents that she felt unreal, she wanted to stay in bed so that it would all seem like a bad dream from which she'd wake up. And when we do, when we finally come out of hiding and take off our masks, we will ask: Who are we? What's happened to us? Is this the beginning of the end, or a new beginning? What do we do now?

In 1838, Abraham Lincoln, an unknown twenty-eight-year-old state legislator, gave a speech in Springfield, Illinois, on "the perpetuation of our political institutions." A quarter century before he led the country through its first near-death experience, Lincoln asked: How might American democracy die? He predicted that no foreign conqueror at the head of a huge army would ever cross the Blue Ridge Mountains and drink from the Ohio River. "If destruction be our lot, we must ourselves be its author and finisher," Lincoln said. "As a nation of freemen, we must live through all time, or die by suicide."

One night, my headlights caught a rectangular flash of red on the roadside by the farm next door to where I'm writing this, in the house where we were lucky to escape the plague. Five white letters stretched across a sign—or signs, for there were two, one planted by the goat pasture's wire fence, another across the road along the hayed field. The blaring shade of that red instantly told me what the five letters said. Two weeks before the election, our neighbors decided to make their preference known. As was their democratic right. They've lived here a whole lot longer than we have. The husband had just dropped off two bales of hay that I needed to mulch fall grass seed; their daughter often sets aside two dozen eggs for us in her roadside farm stand; my wife baked a tray of muffins when the other wife was sick. We all want to be good neighbors.

But the headlights caught something dark, baleful. The sight made me shudder, and for a second I imagined an evil shape in a far more serious red and black. I pushed the image away—don't exaggerate! But what if we were living in another time and country? Then wasn't it thinkable? How long could any hateful ruler stay in power without the approval of good neighbors?

My children were confused and upset. My wife was appalled. I spent the rest of the night trying to connect the red signs out on the road with the decent people who had put them there. I couldn't—I can't.

Our neighbors are committed citizens. The wife served on our town board, and then she ran for town supervisor. She got my vote, in spite of our differing politics, because she's our neighbor, because she cares deeply about her hometown, because government at this level should be nonpartisan, and because I want to preserve a sphere of life where the country's cold civil war can't invade and lay waste to everything. When all the absentee ballots were counted, our neighbor lost by a few score votes. And she lost in part because of people like us, city people who had moved their registration here to swing the district from red to blue because they were angry about the previous presidential election. It was not hard to imagine our neighbors' bitterness at seeing their town changed, their values challenged, and the wife's path blocked by self-certain outsiders without deep roots or high stakes.

But when I went over to their house to talk about it, she expressed no bitterness. She took her loss as God's will. Soon afterward she was appointed a county election commissioner.

In the summer of 2020, signs for local candidates appeared by the wire fence along our neighbors' goat pasture. They were red and white and blue, all-American. For weeks that was it, and I began to hope that would be it. Then, after the first frost, with the pumpkins piling up and darkness coming down earlier every day, the red signs suddenly appeared.

The next morning my family and I went into town on the first day of early voting. There at the front door of the county government building was the wife of the family next door, the election commissioner, dressed up in high heels and greeting voters. Above her mask she was smiling with her eyes. She wanted to let us bring our dog inside and apologized for not being allowed. Rumors of ballot fraud and nullification plots were filthying the air all over the country, but I trusted her integrity. She was an essential worker, making self-government possible. We exchanged the friendliest greetings. I forgot all about the signs.

We never talked about them and never will. Being good neighbors makes the conversation impossible. If we waded into policies and personalities we would soon find ourselves over our heads in the deep water of beliefs and values. We might have to acknowledge that we each saw the other's view as a threat to the country, a gun aimed at the heart of the American way of life and all we hold sacred. After that, how would we be able to wave when they drove by our fence in their Kubota?

But this evasion of talk—it solves nothing. It's part of the collapse.

Self-government is democracy in action—not just rights, laws, and institutions, but what free people *do* together, the habits and skills that enable us to run our own affairs. Tocqueville described self-government as an "art" that needs to be learned. It's what Americans no longer know how to do, or even want to do together. It's hard work, for it needs not just ballots and newspapers and official documents, which we still have, but also trust, which we've lost. It depends on the ability to argue, persuade, and compromise in order to achieve things for the common good, like the suppression of a catastrophic pandemic. It requires you to imagine the experience of others, to recognize their autonomy, and yet to think for yourself.

There's nothing natural about it. You might need a few centuries to learn how to do it and just a few years to forget. "Men will do almost anything but govern themselves," Walter Lippmann wrote a century ago. "They don't want the responsibility." Think of all the ways we avoid it: by raising perfect children, by paying no attention, by finding ways to make more money, by caring for the self's thousand needs, by building an online presence, by letting others do the thinking, by following a demagogue.

Self-government is a practice based on an idea, and that idea is the thing that holds together this sprawling, incomprehensible nation. "The fear of conflicting and irreconcilable interiors, and the lack of a common skeleton, knitting all close, continually haunts me," Walt Whitman wrote in *Democratic Vistas*, his post–Civil War manifesto. "For, I say, the true nationality of the States, the genuine union, when we come to a moral crisis, is, and is to be, after all, neither the written law, nor, (as is generally supposed), either self-interest, or common pecuniary or material objects—but the fervid and tremendous IDEA, melting everything else with resistless heat, and solving all lesser and definite distinctions in vast, indefinite, spiritual emotional power."

Any idea is a fragile thing, even—especially!—a fervid and tremendous one. We should have taken better care of ours.

Look outside. Our bridges are buckling, another factory has closed up, badly ventilated schools are failing to educate another generation of children, hospital beds are overflowing again, local shops are posting out-of-business signs while Amazon delivery trucks fill the streets, our thought leaders sound like carnival barkers, our citizenry seems to be suffering through early-stage National Cognitive Decline, and the common skeleton is unknitting and likely to fall apart in a heap of bones for future archaeologists to study with furrowed expressions of puzzled sadness. Why did exhausted election officials across the country have to stay up late night after night to kill off the thousands of lies spreading through sophisticated digital pathways that were invented by the country's most brilliant and successful entrepreneurs and channeled into millions of minds that have grown strangely vulnerable to contagion? Something has gone wrong with the last best hope of earth. Americans know it—the whole world knows it. Something has gone wrong out there, too.

And yet our civilization is stubbornly persistent. I have the sense that a country this big and powerful could continue in the same way indefinitely without sinking or even changing its course. That worries me as much as national suicide. America can pass through mass death, mass protests, hurricanes, wildfires, hourly scandals, heart-stopping elections, blizzards of lies—but Netflix still streams a new series every week, parents keep paying top dollar for test-prep tutors, Black Friday will be huge this year, and Big Ten football must go on. The engine that powers this behemoth is cutting out, but the vessel keeps moving ahead on the momentum of its own mass and speed.

Americans are usually too comforted by our stable creed and distracted by the flash of novelties to look hard at ourselves. Only a few times in history have we been forced to doubt the survival of self-government. It takes a very large shock to alert us that the engine room has gone silent. A shock on the scale of 2020.

But when I say last best hope, don't misunderstand me. America is no longer a light unto the nations. It was always a role that made us appear better and worse than we were. What do we see in the mirror now? An unstable country, political institutions that might not be perpetuated, a people divided into warring tribes and prone to violence—the kind of country we used to think we could save. No one is going to save us. We are our last best hope.

STRANGE DEFEAT

The year 2020 began with an impeachment trial, the third in American history. The president had used his official powers to extort a political favor from a foreign leader in order to help his own reelection. His guilt was clear—only the tribal loyalty of his party kept him in office. But before long hardly anyone remembered the impeachment.

The year ended with the president's attempt to overturn the results of an election in which 158 million Americans voted, the most ever, and rejected him by a margin of 7 million votes. Holed up in his palace, surrounded by sycophants, he broadcast frantic claims of fraud and victory, while his allies manipulated the levers of government and media to keep him in power, or else maintained a prudent silence, and his deluded followers poured into the streets and websites. If he could have provoked a military coup on his own behalf, he wouldn't have hesitated. If he'd then abolished future elections, millions of Americans would have cheered him. The last day of 2020 came on January 6, 2021, the day that the president sent 20,000 maddened Americans to overthrow self-government.

Up to the very end, what kept Donald Trump from reaching the exalted status of dictator—feared by his bitterest critics, desired by his most fanatic supporters—was his own ineptitude, along with our creaky institutions and the remaining democratic faith of the American people. There was always a perverse comfort in imagining Trump as a fascist, a Mussolini. It would mean that we were up against something clear-cut, both familiar and foreign, as if half the country had come under an alien spell that the other half had somehow resisted. Trump himself encouraged the analogy—the cocked chin, the jutting lower lip, the dramatic way he climbed the floodlit White House balcony steps after being released from Walter Reed Hospital and removed his mask and saluted. The superman restored to full strength.

These images made him seem artificial, more like a European ruler than an American president. But Trump was a native son, an all-American flimflam man and demagogue, a traditional character of our way of life. Twain would have immediately recognized him. He was spawned in a gold-plated sewer with other creatures of our celebrity trash culture: investment gurus, talk-show hosts, evangels of the Prosperity Gospel, surgery-altered TV housewives, bling-worshiping rappers. His supporters are part of us, too. Yes, I'm aware that we've become two countries—but each one continually makes the other. A failure the size of Trump took the whole of America.

The year 2020 saw the most flagrant attempt to subvert democracy since Fort Sumter. It began with attempted blackmail and ended with attempted sedition. Between them was everything else.

When the virus came here, it found a country with serious underlying conditions, and it exploited them ruthlessly. Chronic ills—a corrupt political class, a sclerotic bureaucracy, a heartless economy, a divided and distracted public—had gone untreated for years. We had learned to live, uncomfortably, with the symptoms. It took the scale and intimacy of a pandemic to expose their severity—to shock Americans with the recognition that we are in the high-risk category.

In certain ways the United States was favorably positioned to come through without heavy losses. We had two months to learn from the horrors of China, Iran, and Italy. We are among world leaders in biotechnology, sophisticated hospital equipment, intensive-care capacity, and medical specialists. We live spread out across a vast and rich country, where many people live in single-family houses with grassy yards and commute alone in cars rather than in crowded trains and buses. Our cities are less dense than those of Europe and Asia. And Americans pride themselves on being independent and resourceful in a crisis. The same spirit that drove Clara Barton, a government clerk with no training in health care, to bring medical supplies and comforting words to wounded Union soldiers in Washington at the start of the Civil War would carry Americans through the plague of COVID-19.

Here finally was a crisis that could pull Americans together as hadn't happened in the two decades since September 11, 2001. The biology of a pandemic is designed to show the limits of individualism and affirm a truth that's too hard to keep in mind—our common humanity. Everyone is vulnerable. Everyone's health depends on the health and behavior of others. No one is safe unless everyone takes responsibility for everyone else. No community or region can withstand the plague without an active national government. No country can end it alone.

Generosity and courage broke out everywhere. A planeload of medical workers flew from Atlanta to New York to help in overwhelmed hospitals. General Electric aerospace workers in Massachusetts demanded that their factory be converted to producing ventilators. A hospital television show donated protective equipment that real hospitals lacked. Volunteers ran shopping errands for the sick and elderly or took out their sewing machines to stitch masks. The dedication of New York's nurses and doctors inspired residents across the city to come to their windows at the nightly seven o'clock shift change and bang pots and cheer and sing to the nearly empty streets. Just staying home and making yourself tolerable to your family was a patriotic act.

And yet, despite all this, the United States quickly became the world leader in infections and deaths, far beyond its share of the global population—a position it held throughout the year. Technological prowess and individual sacrifice were no match for national incoherence. The virus exploited every fault line, every division of class, race, geography, and politics, every declining social and economic indicator, every institutional weakness, every blind spot and bias. The failure began at the top, where it was least forgivable and most devastating, but it extended to the whole society.

Just after the fall of France in the summer of 1940, the French historian, soldier, and future Resistance fighter Marc Bloch wrote a short book called *Strange Defeat*. He described how years of declining national solidarity and cultural decay had preceded the French collapse before the German invaders. The failure belonged to every sector—the military, the bourgeoisie, political parties, trade unions, schools, and universities. Bloch didn't spare his own profession. "The staffs worked with tools which were put into their hands by the nation at large," he wrote of the military high command. "They could be only what the totality of the social *fact*, as it existed in France, permitted them to be."

Like France in 1940, America in 2020 stunned itself with a collapse that was larger and deeper than one leader. Under invasion and occupation, few of our institutions held up. So we have to ask: What is the totality of the social fact as it exists in America?

Start with the landscape that lay open to the virus. In the

prosperous cities, a class of globally connected desk workers dependent on a class of precarious service workers. In the countryside, decaying communities in reaction against the modern world. On media, endless vituperation among different camps. In the economy, even with full employment, a large and growing gap between triumphant capital and beleaguered labor. In Washington, a hollow government led by a con man and his morally bankrupt party. Around the country, a mood of cynical exhaustion, with no vision of a shared identity or future.

A crisis as massive and new as a pandemic brings an almost inevitable failure of imagination. It was hard at first to believe that the pictures of deserted streets and chaotic hospitals in other countries had anything to do with us. The solidity of everyday life was comforting, and dangerous. When the virus began to spread here, no one knew what to do. The authorities gave confused instructions or none at all. Families and organizations were left to make their decisions alone: go on riding the train, keep the office open, send the kids to school, visit friends? Or cancel everything, buy the last rolls of toilet paper, and take shelter? Americans woke up every morning to a feeling that was for many of us—though not all—radically new: our government didn't care if we died. It felt as if we were living in a failed state.

Those early days reminded me of experiences I've had in other countries, like Iraq or Sierra Leone, where the state is too weak or indifferent to take care of its citizens, where the leaders are too corrupt or stupid to head off mass suffering.

People unlucky enough to live in such places don't expect the government to place any value on their lives. They have to look after themselves, so they ignore official statements, share the latest rumors, barricade their streets, and pool money to keep teachers in schools and doctors in clinics. Here, of course, government continued to perform its basic functions. Police answered 911 calls, social security checks came in the mail. But the sense that we were on our own never went away all year. There was no national plan for dealing with the greatest threat of our lives. Every time Trump spoke in public, the knot in the stomach tightened.

On March 6, Trump toured the laboratories of the Centers for Disease Control and Prevention outside Atlanta. Wearing a golf jacket and a red "Keep America Great" campaign hat, flanked by doctors and political allies, the president paused for forty-five minutes with the press and played an epidemiologist who's pleased with his lab results. He kept returning to the low American numbers—240 confirmed cases, 11 deaths—as if they would stay put if we just stopped testing and kept sick passengers from leaving an offshore cruise ship. Trump was in a jocular mood. "I like this stuff, I really get it," he said. "People are really surprised I understand this stuff. Every one of these doctors said, 'How do you know so much about this?' Maybe I have a natural ability."

Dr. Robert Redfield, the director of the CDC with the white Amish beard, stood next to Trump, hands behind his back, mouth half-open, nervously eyeing the president sideways as if he might suddenly do something unpredictable.

Redfield remained silent when Trump declared, among other lies, "Anybody that wants a test can get a test."

Heidi Klum, the model and reality-TV host, got a test after complaining to her 7 million Instagram followers that she couldn't. The entire roster of the Brooklyn Nets got tests. Trump's family, friends, donors, and allies got tests after being exposed at a birthday party and a political conference. Celebrities, athletes, the wealthy and well-connected—some of them with no symptoms—could always get tests. An Internet joke proposed that the only way to find out whether you had the virus was to sneeze in a rich person's face. But nurses, police officers, and thousands of ordinary Americans with fevers and dry coughs could not get tests. In New York and Seattle and California they waited in long and possibly infectious lines, only to be turned away if they weren't actually suffocating. Because there were nowhere near enough tests.

Grotesque inequality—that was an essential piece of the social fact of America in 2020. Before the pandemic it had become completely natural for privileged people to be allowed to cut to the front of the line. That these stories managed to spark outrage showed that the crisis was deep enough to force Americans out of thoughtless acceptance and into a state of awareness that can be a condition of change.

It's shocking now to look at the video of Trump's March 6 visit to the CDC. The president struts his mastery, the government doctors flatter him, and the politicians smile, smug and clueless. Redfield talks about a strategy of "containment," but it's too late. The virus was already infiltrating

New York City's apartment buildings and office towers and subways. The next day, Governor Andrew Cuomo declared a state of emergency; within two weeks, New York and California would shut down; by the end of the month, New York City would have its thousandth COVID death. Everyone standing with Trump amid the machines and wires in the white fluorescent light of the lab was complicit in a grand deception. They were denying Americans a chance to protect themselves while they had time.

The country's political class responded to the crisis incoherently, and in some cases treacherously. The behavior of leaders charged with the general welfare was so destructive that it revealed more than ordinary incompetence. The pressure of the pandemic showed how little was left of public service and national unity even as ideals. In their place grew malignancy.

At best, politicians who took the plague seriously waited too long to act or made initial mistakes that caused thousands of deaths. Until the middle of March, the mayor of New York City told people to go on with their lives and keep sending their children by bus and subway to schools where they sneezed, coughed, and touched noses, mouths, doorknobs, and one another. The governor of New York State ordered hospitalized elderly patients back into their nursing homes, which quickly formed the worst clusters of infection, and then he concealed the extent of the tragedy.

At worst, leaders used their positions to benefit themselves while leaving the public to its fate. In January and February, while the president was telling Americans that the virus was under control and would soon disappear, a handful of donors, investors, and U.S. senators—among them Kelly Loeffler of Georgia, the newest and richest member of the Senate—received alarming private briefings from the administration: the virus was highly aggressive, nothing like the flu, and not under control. They quickly traded stocks on the information while publicly saying nothing about the danger they knew was coming, or even giving false assurances that would be certain to get people killed. In the White House, the president's son-in-law, Jared Kushner, took over the pandemic response and advocated playing down the threat out of concern for the stock market and his father-in-law's re-election. He interfered in the work of more competent officials, compromised security protocols, dabbled in conflicts of interest, flirted with violations of federal law, and then promised nationwide testing through his business connections, which never materialized.

None of this cost anyone's position, or was even all that surprising. The American people have grown used to parasites attaching themselves at the top of our democracy and sucking its lifeblood. Sexting with a staffer does more harm to a politician than profiteering in a national crisis.

Kushner and Loeffler: mirror images, elongated, slim-suited, self-seeking dilettantes who entered politics at the highest level because of wealth they never had to earn. Kushner gained admission to Harvard and New York University through his father's multimillion-dollar donations, married into another fortune, became a slumlord, failed in both newspaper publishing and real estate, then was made a senior White House advisor with expertise in nothing. Loeffler married her financier boss, became a major donor to the Republican Party, was paid back by the governor of Georgia with an empty Senate seat, and joined the president's smiling entourage at the CDC. By then she had remade herself from a suburban moderate into a liberal-baiting, gun-playing extremist. Kushner and Loeffler were fraudulent meritocrats who became fake populists when it served their interests. Their biographies tell the story of an entire era's decline.

Tocqueville found that the most striking thing about American democracy, the central fact from which all his other observations sprang, was "the equality of conditions." He didn't mean equal results, which, given the diversity of human talents and pursuits, could only be imposed by a state that made some more equal than others. He meant equal status in society—the desire to be no one's inferior. This "passion for equality" (even as it excluded the enslaved, indigenous, and female inhabitants of America, a parenthesis almost as big as the country) was stronger than the love of freedom. "Freedom," Tocqueville wrote, "is not the chief and continual object of their desires; it is equality for which they feel an eternal love." Americans would rather give up their political liberty than their feeling of being equals. "They will put up with poverty, servitude, and barbarism, but they will not endure aristocracy."

Trump reached the White House on the strength of this insight. He offered his supporters a deal: they would give him unprecedented powers, even the power to decide for them what was true; in exchange, he would drag the elites down and elevate his supporters as "the people." He would give them equality in servitude to him. Trump's inherited wealth and garish lifestyle didn't invalidate him as a populist tribune in their eyes, as progressives thought it should. Money alone doesn't violate the American idea of equality—what offends ordinary people is being looked down on by those with unwarranted power and privilege. Trump got a pass because he articulated the essence of his people's condition, which was resentment. Its taste was in his mouth, too.

Populism is the politics of "the people" turned against "the elites." It's inherent in democracies, always lurking, and it grows out of control when citizens feel that their needs are going unmet or their voices unheard. Then they will revolt against the class above them that claims to rule by right of superior knowledge and seems to do so for its own benefit. The experts—civil servants, trade negotiators, think tank analysts, scientists, professors, journalists—have a tenuous hold on their status, if not their jobs. No one elected them. They're unaccountable to the mass public. The same credentials and special language that make them recognizable and admirable to one another render them suspect in the eyes of the noncredentialed.

At the start of the pandemic, the experts made crucial mistakes that haunted them for the rest of the year. The entire purpose of the CDC, with its eleven thousand highly educated employees and $7 billion budget, was to track and contain the spread of such a virus, but the agency lost months failing to develop a test on a scale large enough to do it. Technical glitches contributed to this failure, but so did bureaucratic rigidity and a cautious mindset, made worse by layers of rules imposed by Congress in the years after 9/11.

In the past two decades the permanent government has suffered from the general inflammation of politics. The morale of civil servants plummeted as their budgets were used as political weapons, freezes and furloughs became routine, and demagogic politicians set them up as targets for their own failures with terms of abuse such as "unelected bureaucrats." The public came to associate civil servants with the rampant corruption of the federal government—in Trump's language, "the swamp"—when in reality most are lifers working toward a pension, with no revolving doors to spin through and no way to cash in, a squeezed class of workers in wildly prosperous and expensive Washington.

Civil servants have lost their status, and with it their willingness to take initiative. They've come to be treated like well-educated clerks whose main concern is to avoid controversy with their political masters while doing their jobs.

They are knowledgeable in a specialized area, conscientious, risk-averse, snowed in paperwork, and increasingly under-paid compared with their peers in the private sector. Trump saw the federal government as property he'd acquired by winning the election, and civil servants as his personal em-ployees. Any other commitment on their part—to the coun-try, the Constitution, or the facts—was rank disloyalty. He imagined scheming conspirators in drab D.C. office wear, coup plotters hidden in plain sight at desks, in lunchrooms, and on jogging paths around the federal capital: the "deep state." He set about bending it to his will and purging the "traitors."

Meanwhile, out in the country, the public health sys-tem that treats widespread illnesses such as diabetes, venereal disease, and addiction has been hollowed out for years. In the decade after the Great Recession, spending on local and state departments was cut by 15 percent, eliminating 55,000 jobs, a quarter of the national workforce. Public and private spending on advanced medical research remained high, while the country's front-line defenses were abandoned—one more casualty of the iron law of inequality. All of this helps to explain why a country that would go on to produce a miraculous vaccine in less than a year had such a hard time testing, tracing, and caring for its people.

And so, as the pandemic shut down cities and states, half the country looked to science and the other half looked to Trump. Americans didn't look to one another because there was no longer any trust between them. Into this void government by the people collapsed, leaving the unelected elites and the elected demagogue to battle it out. The struggle continued all year, breaking the country along one of its most tender fracture lines—the culture of expertise and the culture of populism. A healthier society might have mustered the solidarity that can emerge in the face of a common threat. Citizens of Taiwan, New Zealand, Rwanda, and Norway all responded this way—not because they trust science more than others, but because they trust one another and their government more.

In mid-March the president suddenly sprang into action and declared a national emergency. For a few minutes he took to calling himself a wartime leader. But the leader he brought to mind was Marshal Philippe Pétain, the French general who, in 1940, signed an armistice with German invaders after the rout of French forces, then formed the pro-Nazi Vichy regime and abandoned his country to prolonged disaster. Trump's only interest was himself and his hold on power. So, when essential medical equipment—even masks— remained scarce due to depleted stockpiles and scrapped plans, he blamed the Obama administration. When his son-in-law's idea of using private business to replace the national government in testing and production bombed, he blamed the governors of the most afflicted states, who happened to be Democrats. When Russia, Taiwan, and the United Nations sent humanitarian aid to the world's richest power—

a beggar nation in utter chaos—he withdrew the United States from the World Health Organization. When his own experts gave accurately bleak assessments, he insulted and then silenced them.

"WE CANNOT LET THE CURE BE WORSE THAN THE PROBLEM ITSELF," Trump tweeted in late March. He wasn't wrong. Both containing the virus and fending off ruin were priorities for a decent society, which would have to negotiate the trade-off between them. But Americans couldn't do it, because half the country assumed—correctly—that Trump was looking after his own interests and could never be trusted to look out for the common good. So some Americans closed their ears to the anger and desperation of other Americans who were demanding an end to the lockdown, and who in turn refused to contain the viral peril. This was the fatal logic of polarization.

In April, as case numbers exploded into hundreds of thousands and deaths into tens of thousands, Trump abandoned any pretense of managing the crisis and settled into the natural response of a demagogue. A deep instinct told him that his best bet for survival was to divide up the country. He had staked his short political career on the American people's readiness to turn on one another, and they had not let him down. With his inerrant knack for driving Americans into frenzies of mutual hatred, he scoffed at mask wearing. In other countries masks were an everyday device for keeping others and yourself from harm, like sneezing into your arm or wearing a seat belt. In the United States they became the most potent weapon in the civil war between Democrats and Republicans, experts and populists. You could immediately tell whether a crowd was blue or red by the presence or absence of masks. Not to wear one became a badge of political identity. And because our country is more a whole than we think, to wear one did as well.

Nothing Trump did was more destructive than turning the pandemic into a central front of the partisan war. How many of the hundreds of thousands of American dead would be breathing today if he had told the whole country to wear a mask?

The anti-maskers—a minority, but a large one—used the language of freedom. But freedom no longer means what Tocqueville intended by it—the art of self-government through the use of free institutions. To the anti-maskers it meant almost the opposite: the absence of any obstacle that got in the way of what they wanted. "Free Ohio!" they chanted in Columbus. In Lansing they blocked traffic and waved signs that said, "Pro–Common Sense, Anti-Tyranny" and, from the eighteenth century, "Don't Tread on Me." The protesters ranged from the sympathetic to the intimidating. They spoke about shuttered businesses, delayed unemployment checks, faith in God, gun rights, Trump 2020, creeping socialism, the Gates-Soros global conspiracy, and the fake-news media. ("In New York City the hospitals are *not* overloaded." "We're being lied to!") They had their own facts as well as their own principles, which came down to their constitutional right to risk getting people killed.

The maskers had opposing rhetoric and values. Instead of raucous protests in the streets, they aired their pleas and rebukes on social media and modeled their views by strapping a piece of cloth across their faces. They invoked public health, the common good, and the names of the dead. The communitarians answered the rage of the individualists with quieter anger, righteous disgust, and appeals to data and expertise. "Follow the science!" became their mantra. Or, at most: "Wear the damn mask!" Actual persuasion across this divide was rare. It usually required an extraordinary circumstance.

In one of the worst weeks of the pandemic, a nurse in El Paso named Ashley Bartholomew was completing her shift in the COVID intensive care unit. A patient who had begun to recover was watching TV—a story about El Paso's critical need for refrigerated morgue trucks. Suddenly he said, "Fake news. I don't think COVID is really more than a flu."

"Now you think differently, though?" Bartholomew asked, unsure what he meant.

"No, the same," the patient said. "I should just take vitamins for my immune system. They're making it a big deal."

The nurse didn't know what to say. She was wrapped in protective gear. The ICU was overflowing. All around her were the sick and dying. At the end of her shift she was going to resign her job out of sheer exhaustion. Ordinarily she never spoke about other patients to one in her care, but now something made her do it.

"To be honest, this is my last shift," the nurse said.

"You're the only patient of twenty-five that has been able to speak to me today, or is even aware I'm here."

"Really?" The patient remained skeptical. He asked if many of her patients had died. She told him that she'd given CPR to more of them in the past two weeks than throughout her ten years as a nurse.

The man's tone changed, and he said he was sorry. The nurse began to cry. Tears ran down under her glasses, her mask, her respirator, and her face shield, onto her gown. She apologized for losing her composure.

As she brought the man out of the ICU to a unit with a lower level of care, they passed some of the patients she'd told him about. Later, while they were waiting for another nurse, the man said, "Thank you for telling me what you told me. I saw a lot of the other ones when you were wheeling me out of the ICU. It's much more than a flu. I was mistaken."

Bartholomew thanked him and hoped for his total recovery.

"I will tell everyone who denies how bad this is about my experiences," he said.

One mind changed—but this patient in intensive care had to hear the truth from a devastated nurse who summoned the will to make him think about others. Then he had to see for himself. Some patients refused to believe it was real until their last breaths. Some not even then.

It didn't matter what the experts said. The populists refused to believe them *because* they were experts, as protective of their status as any other group. And the experts had sometimes been wrong. A COVID denier could point to the early testing debacle at the CDC, and the confused messages on social distancing, masks, and asymptomatic transmission, to argue that the experts had their heads up their asses. Without a shared reality, every data point, every body count just proves its opposite, like a knot getting tighter the harder you try to undo it. Once politics becomes an identity clash or tribal war, a death spiral can set in that's very hard to escape. Aided by information technology, which gives everyone all the reality of their own that they could want, this epistemic rupture is more powerful than personal experience, monetary interest, or even the fervid and tremendous IDEA. Democracy's survival depends on what happens inside our skulls, where anything is possible. The destruction of a shared reality does more damage than economic decline or impeachable acts.

The scientists were right about this: there was no way to save lives and jobs except by ending the pandemic, and no way to end it except by a fast and hard lockdown. The way of "freedom"—letting people decide for themselves whether or not to wear masks inside crowded bars that were allowed to stay open—made the tragedy far worse in places like South Dakota, which should have benefited from a sparse population and ample warning. But a yearlong pitched battle between experts and populists during a once-a-century pandemic was a different kind of tragedy.

"Follow the science" doesn't tell a society where to go, because it leaves out politics. Experts know things that the rest of us have to hear, but they can't be our rulers. Siloed in their separate fields and committed to their different visions, they can't weigh the arguments of epidemiologists against those of economists and child psychiatrists and come up with a policy for the common good. In a democracy only the people can do that, through their government. But the people were divided, and the government was incompetent and malevolent. When it failed, each half of the country drove the other into absolutist positions and self-caricatures.

"Our government leaders have abandoned me!" a Michigan restaurant owner shouted at a local news reporter, approaching the camera with a finger extended. He was going to defy the governor's order to close down. "There was enough money to give every family in this country twenty thousand dollars to go home for two months. They chose to give it to special interests and campaign donors." The reporter (unmasked) asked if it was right to violate a state order. "State order!" the restaurant owner (unmasked) spat. "This isn't an order, this is a conspiracy! This is a tyranny!" In thirty seconds he lost whatever support he'd just won from viewers who believed in science.

In the worst days of the lockdown I had nothing but contempt for people like him. They were irrational and criminally selfish. When they yelled about individual rights it meant they were pissed off because they couldn't go out for barbecue and beer or have their roots colored. And how much did they really care about freedom? They had surrendered theirs to Trump.

There's a photograph of a group of protesters outside the Ohio statehouse in Columbus, where the governor was giving his daily press briefing. Trump hats, American flags, a Guy Fawkes mask, enraged faces pressed against the windows, mouths open as wide as in *The Scream*—you can almost see the spray of viral aerosols misting the glass. They're making themselves ugly—morally ugly. Some wags likened them to zombies howling for flesh. It became the most famous image of the anti-lockdown protests, and it foreshadowed the more dramatic photographs at the national Capitol.

I clicked on the photo during an Internet search. I had a lot of time for Internet searches in 2020. Like tens of millions of the locked-down, I spent hours every day sitting on my ass, staring at a screen. This posture—spine curving, hands scrubbed red and splayed across a keyboard, eyes narrowing at the pixelated glow—identified me as a nonessential worker.

This was a new category in our economic organization. Writers, architects, accountants, managers, lawyers, bankers, programmers, professors, U.S. senators: nonessential. Highly educated and rewarded, but not the most important people in a crisis. Sixty percent of college graduates were able to work from home, compared with just 15–20 percent of high school grads. I worked from home, I learned to hate Zoom, I kept my job, my family and I were OK. Many of the protesters, like the Michigan restaurant owner, were not OK, but I was too angry to hear the pain coming out of their screaming mouths. In that dark and frightening time they weren't restaurant owners, hairdressers, and contractors whose life savings were disappearing. They were Trump's people, stupid and cruel. They waved obnoxious signs and partisan banners and in some cases semi-automatics. They made it too easy not to listen.

My attitude had something to do with my good luck. My life savings were doing pretty well. I was comfortable and I was afraid, and this fearful security shut down my imaginative sympathy. No wonder they resented me as much as I despised them.

Who were the essential workers? Health care personnel, of course, but also shelf stockers, Instacart shoppers, farmers, meat processors, municipal employees, home health aides, warehouse workers, long-haul truckers. Doctors and nurses were the combat heroes, but the supermarket cashier with her bottle of sanitizer and the UPS driver with his latex gloves were the supply and logistics troops who kept the frontline forces intact. Essential workers were the ones we couldn't live without, who couldn't stay home, who toiled in the physical world. For the most part they're the American working class. And to deskbound, Internet-addicted professionals who enjoy the softest working conditions in human history, they are all but invisible.

The industrial age produced—along with brutal jobs, disfiguring accidents, and child labor—a heroic image of the factory worker: physically powerful, his face smudged with coal dust or scorched by the blast furnace, oppressed by the work but not its total victim. He was coiled with energy that was frightening to some and inspiring to others—the same violent strength could be applied to the machine at hand or to the battle for wages and dignity. The industrial worker filled the popular imagination in news stories, books, movies, and even popular songs, putting a grimy human face on capitalism while dramatizing the social changes and conflicts it brought. For half a century he had the country's fate in his muscular hands at the center of a great national drama—the fight for economic security.

As the industrial age waned, the hero of labor became the working stiff, paying dues to a sluggish union, bored and trapped by his job, but still able to take its existence for granted, like the Chicago steelworker who opens Studs Terkel's 1974 oral history, *Working*. He isn't afraid to ask his abusive foreman, "Who the hell are you, Hitler?" Those were the last years of secure blue-collar work, and the beginning of wage stagnation in the postindustrial service economy. The archetype of the new working class was the Walmart store greeter: fifty or fifty-five years old, having lost a better-paying factory job, making ten dollars an hour, in poor physical shape, on her feet all day, forced to be cheerful with the shopping public. She was isolated, anxious, and basically powerless, under the constant threat of having her hours reduced or losing her job outright, since the skill bar was low and someone always needed the work. Of course, no union protected her, not even a corrupt one.

There is no heroic image of this working class. The dignity of labor isn't extended to nursing home attendants. Target scanners don't march in Labor Day parades. Their work involves more contact with the consuming public than manufacturing, but in a way service workers are less seen, less *imagined* by desk workers than their industrial predecessors were. The human encounter with floor associates and cream cheese schmearers is brief, maybe annoying, maybe even a little embarrassing, for it reminds you how many jobs in the low-price, low-wage economy are crappy ones. The encounter requires an instant act of forgetting.

Then came one-click shopping on Amazon, and the encounter disappeared altogether. Instead of an unhappy cashier with her wrist in a splint, you are confronted with a button that says "BUY" and then, a day or two later, a cardboard box at your door with a smile on its side. The chain of events in between takes a conscious effort to bring to mind. It's hard even to picture an Amazon worker (because of the company's secrecy there aren't many photographs to help your imagination). It's easy to forget she exists. Along with the immense convenience and efficiency of the smartphone economy, this erasure is part of what makes it so seductive. "Seamless" means inhuman.

The early stage of the pandemic brought a great change. Almost overnight, an entire class became visible to the rest of society—the essential workers who rang up groceries, stocked shelves, and delivered goods. The consuming public learned where its food came from and who kept it alive, involuntarily picturing the hands that butchered hogs and packaged books and carried the box with the smile on its side. The masked and gloved delivery driver, watched through the kitchen window, might be the only human being who came to the house. These weren't just essential workers, they were "heroes." If they didn't show up people would die, but by showing up they risked dying. Their struggles became news. A Bay Area package sorter went to work with a feeling of broken glass in her throat because she feared ending up homeless. An assistant manager at an infected Amazon warehouse on Staten Island was fired for leading a walkout after symptomatic colleagues had to keep working in order to be paid. "They're in this building, getting sick," he said. "And the people making all the money are comfortable off the grid somewhere, and they're getting on TV and they're saying everything is fine while we're in the trenches. Jeff Bezos can kiss my ass."

An essential worker was a worker who would be fired for staying home with symptoms of the virus. Think about it enough and you realize that the miraculous price and speed of a delivery of organic microgreens from Amazon Fresh to your doorstep depends on the fact that the people who grow, sort, pack, and deliver it have to work while sick. Think some more and you wonder if you'd really accept a higher price and slower delivery so that they could stay home. The underside of the consumer economy—how it implicated everyone—was exposed in all its ugliness.

The divide between the nonessentials at home and the essentials on the job was as wide as that between civilians and soldiers in wartime. If you were a civilian, it was hard not to feel some shame. At the start of the pandemic I had several conversations with an emergency medicine doctor who was treating COVID patients in New York City (and who got sick himself). When I expressed chagrin at having no civic duty except to stay home, he said, "Your job is to stay out of my hospital." That made me feel better for about five minutes.

We were all in this together. That was the message of the public health authorities, and of the virus itself. By staying apart we showed our togetherness. It was an inspiring thought, and it lasted about two weeks. With different leadership it might have lasted longer. But history was against us—plagues usually bring terror, stigma, and ostracism—and the early solidarity soon gave way to the recognition that, far from joining Americans in a common national effort like rationing sugar and buying war bonds, the pandemic was exploiting all our underlying conditions. In theory the virus was a great leveler. In fact it fell with unerring accuracy on Americans who could bear it least. It became a relentless force for inequality.

Westchester and Manhattan suffered first, but Queens and the Bronx suffered most. Black, brown, old, and poor Americans—several generations living together in close quarters with bad ventilation, afflicted with health troubles, deprived of good medical care, obliged to go to work, unaware or distrustful of instructions from on high, rushed too late to overwhelmed hospitals—perished in terrifying numbers. Later on, when the pandemic reached the rural heartland, and second and third waves infected huge numbers in places like Iowa and New Mexico, hospitals in small towns were overwhelmed by the same poverty, the same unhealthy population, the same inadequate care.

At the end of March, Congress passed nearly $4 trillion in relief bills. Given the decade-long coma into which the world's greatest legislative body had fallen—given that Congress no longer did much of anything other than confirm judges to the federal bench and fight over the debt ceiling—this act was a historic achievement, and evidence that a big enough crisis could still shock government into action. By some accounts the stimulus payments and unemployment relief put more money in the hands of desperate people than the New Deal had done. It staved off widespread hunger and homelessness. Another chunk of money saved tens of thousands of small businesses from destruction. But by the end of summer most of the money was gone, while the virus was still very much here. The two parties returned to their customary positions, with Republicans blocking a second round of spending, and millions of Americans faced ruin.

All the economic trends of the years before the pandemic accelerated. Educated professionals, if they suffered any losses, bounced back quickly in both incomes and investments. Those with high school degrees, poorer workers, women, and the young took the biggest hits, with more than 70 million Americans losing jobs. Technology companies prospered, like those in which Kelly Loeffler and other insiders shrewdly invested after they received their early warnings. Economic power became ever more concentrated as monopolies such as Walmart and Target gained enormous shares of the market, while hundreds of thousands of small businesses disappeared. On some New York City streets, four out of five shops closed forever. True to its name, Amazon seemed to engulf everything.

At the same moment unemployment rose to near-Depression levels, the stock market reached a record high. The work economy and the investor economy occupied separate realities. The very rich became much richer—the country's six-hundred-odd billionaires increased their wealth by nearly 50 percent. The richest of them all, Jeff Bezos, added around $70 billion to his net worth, while 20,000 of his employees came down with the virus. Even the relief bills increased inequality, by giving large tax breaks to business owners who might have felt no impact from the pandemic. The social safety net kept ripping, forcing the sick to continue working and mothers to choose between their job and their children, throwing people off health insurance and onto hollowed-out state unemployment systems, whose ancient websites crashed and phones went unanswered under the immense demand. Economists spoke of a "K-shaped recovery." Some Americans rose back rapidly; the rest continued to plummet into poverty.

These trends have been with us since the 1970s, longer than most Americans have been alive. The causes are numbingly familiar. In the past two decades the effects have gathered speed.

The pandemic brought the economy to a temporary standstill. The pause let us see through the usual blur of change to the deeper permanence of our arrangements. In 2020, inequality killed large numbers of Americans. Whatever the arguments about government spending and taxes and regulations, our economic system makes national solidarity in a crisis impossible.

Lack of solidarity turned every hard problem of the pandemic, everything on the society-wide scale of testing or vaccination, into a crisis within a crisis. Competing interests, conflicting values, sclerotic institutions, and general mistrust overwhelmed common purpose and often common sense. Two groups that had no voice of their own seemed to disappear altogether: the old, imprisoned in their homes and facilities, the likeliest to die, and children, who were mostly spared the physical damage of the virus, but not the social havoc. Children had no lobby or union or spokesman to press their interests. Their fate depended on the country's ability to come together around a coherent response. So they were doomed.

In New York the schools stayed open two weeks longer than they should have, even as some teachers stopped coming to class and some parents withdrew their children. The reason given by the mayor and the chancellor was "equity," a word that has recently elbowed aside "equality." Equity, in its current meaning, looks at outcomes, not opportunities, and at groups, not individuals, distinguishing between them based on disparate needs. In this case, poor children needed open schools for meals and safety; poor parents might have no Internet access for online learning at home, no one to care for the kids while they went to work. Equity said to keep the schools open. It was a compelling argument, as long as COVID's viciousness remained unknown. But by March 7, with the city's poorest neighborhoods already becoming the world's leading hot spots, *The New York Times* still reported on the virus as less of a threat than bigotry: "Teachers said that, at this point, they were much more concerned about racism and xenophobia directed at Asian students because of the virus's origins in China than they were with the virus itself." The battle to establish where equity came down plagued American education for the rest of the year.

The schools finally closed in mid-March. After that, our kids spent most of the year in front of computer screens. Again, we were lucky: available laptops, steady Wi-Fi, parents working at home with just enough flexible time to help with studies. But the isolation was demoralizing—the canceled performances, the estrangement from schools and teachers and friends. Technology fans predicted a golden age of learning, with the whole virtual world for a classroom. Maybe adults could adapt to meeting co-workers on Zoom—some might even like it so much that they'd never come back from the Internet—but I knew instinctively that remote learning would mean little or none at all. You had only to be familiar with the glazed depression on the face of a boy who's just surfaced from half a day of gaming, the fierce oblivion of a girl pawing at her social media apps, to understand that the devices would take them away from the world and give too little back. Silicon Valley tech moguls forbid their own children to use them. They know better than anyone the addictive properties that make their inventions so lucrative.

Teachers—essential workers, though they no longer went into school buildings—were as capable of heroism or dereliction as workers in any other sector. But regardless of individual effort, remote education failed our family along with everyone else's, and by June the fragments of the year lay scattered around us. The reports nationwide were dismal. Many children simply stopped showing up online, many others were failing classes, and a whole generation was falling months behind in its education. With urban school districts shut down, Black and Latino students were more likely than white students to be learning remotely, and across the country they were falling behind by almost twice as many months. Wealthier children had access to devices and connections that poor children lacked, they didn't have to look after siblings, they took music lessons on Zoom and joined learning pods with friends. Private schools planned to reopen in the fall, with extra teachers and improved ventilation. Parents who could afford it were pulling their kids out of public schools to salvage their education. The pandemic made the main institution for equal opportunity in America dramatically weaker and less equal.

Over the summer, school districts and teachers' unions discussed whether to reopen schools in September. Studies showed that viral transmission among children was low; a handful of summer programs had started up with few problems; school was about to resume across Europe.

Then Trump, desperate to declare the pandemic over in advance of the election, demanded a reopening of the schools: "It's very important for our country. It's very important for the well-being of the student and the parents. We're going to be putting a lot of pressure on: open your schools in the fall." He threatened to cut off federal funds to schools that stayed shut. Following the political logic of the pandemic, the teachers' unions immediately backed off. The head of the second-largest union spoke dismissively of Trump's "political bullshit." Districts that had been preparing to reopen decided to continue remote education for another semester. Among the big cities, only New York pushed ahead for a partial reopening. For our family, even two days a week in class with strict protocols came as a blessed relief, but it turned out to be short-lived. Across the country, half of white students had the option to go back to school, compared with just a quarter of Black and Latino students. The children faring worst under remote education were condemned to more of it.

By this measure, equity should have said to reopen. But equity turned out to be a slippery concept. In New York, a higher proportion of white families chose the option to send their children back to school than Black families, most of which decided for various reasons to keep their kids home despite the disadvantages. Obedient to the logic of equity, the *Times* cast doubt on whether Mayor de Blasio's bold plan to reopen the schools had been worth the huge effort. When later numbers added up *all* racial groups and showed that the majority of students returning to school were nonwhite, the *Times* reversed its position on reopening. The paper was so tangled up in its own moral dogmas that it couldn't bring itself to make the obvious point: learning in a classroom with a teacher and peers is better for *all* children.

The problem of the schools was hard and urgent. Other than keeping people alive and out of destitution, nothing mattered more than the well-being of children. And yet the country watched an entire year go by while a generation quietly suffered permanent damage. Each group brought ideological battles and professional interests to the crisis and treated other groups as if they were illegitimate. While individual teachers did heroic work both in class and online, their unions defended their collective rights as narrowly as possible and resisted returning to school, defying science, sense, and the welfare of the children to whom they'd supposedly devoted their careers. The Chicago Teachers Union posted a tweet (soon deleted under a barrage of criticism): "The push to reopen schools is rooted in sexism, racism and misogyny." Keeping schools closed became the "progressive" position, even though it was destroying the futures of poor kids. Parents with money and degrees—safely behind their laptop screens—pushed so hard in the opposite direction that they disregarded the legitimate worries of their children's teachers. Democratic governors, against all the data, kept schools closed while opening restaurants and gyms, having more to fear from unions and lobbies than parents and children. Republican governors who opposed any restrictions, including the easiest—masks—presided over outbreaks that spread into schools, all the while accusing Democrats of driving fourteen-year-olds to suicide. Epidemiologists wanted the schools closed for the sake of public health. Pediatricians wanted them open for the sake of children's health. The president wanted to get reelected. Kids were not consulted.

Imagination and initiative were in short supply. New York and other cities could have held school in parks and playgrounds and on blocked-off streets. Unions could have told their underperforming members that more was expected than the minimum in a national disaster. School districts could have hired unemployed people with particular skills to tutor struggling students. Cities, states, and Congress could have dedicated money in an all-out push to reopen. Instead, confronted with an unprecedented problem, every institution stalled, checked its rule book or its contract, and announced that nothing could be done.

Most Americans—the luckier ones—adjusted quietly to the hardships of the pandemic. Everyone complained, but for a nation of road trippers and instant gratifiers there was remarkably little. Our younger child had trouble remembering what her life had been like before. We worried about my ninety-five-year-old mother, in a California nursing home with periodic outbreaks, and about my wife's parents, alone in middle Pennsylvania with dangerously compromised immune systems. Over time we wore down toward a sense of awful normality. The rest of humanity, including other Americans, dissolved in our screens. The grinding isolation made us passive and self-centered. So much for all being in it together—what a long time ago that was!

It was never going to be easy to negotiate the trade-off between the physical health of teachers and the mental health of children, between the guidance of scientists and the livelihood of waiters, between being alive and being OK. All of this required a society where people encountered one another as fellow citizens of goodwill and a government that heard them, and we had neither.

When protests exploded in late spring in Minneapolis, across the country, and around the world, they had nothing directly to do with the pandemic. They were sparked by an 8-minute 46-second video of a Black man being crushed to death by the knee of a criminally depraved policeman. The protests lasted for days, then weeks, then months, and in some places they never ended. In this country, 7 million or 15 million or 26 million people participated—it's impossible to know the number, there were too many gatherings and they were too big—in 2,500 towns and cities. Around the world, people protested in at least 70 countries. There was a protest in Vidor, Texas, a town with a notorious Klan history, where white people knelt and bowed their heads in silence. White protesters joined others in immense numbers, flowing down Flatbush Avenue from Grand Army Plaza in a river of bicycles thousands strong to show concern for their Black compatriots—"White Silence = Violence," "Black Trans Lives Matter." There had never been anything like the protests that followed the killing of George Floyd. They were the largest in our history.

The unrest took me by complete surprise. We were three months into the pandemic, and the 100,000th American had just died. It felt as if a long silence was suddenly broken by a cry of rage out in the street. It wasn't the cry I expected—it wasn't fury at leaders, starting with Trump, who had contributed to mass suffering and shocking racial disparities in rates of hospitalization and death. The protests took us back to the time before the pandemic, when videos of violence against Black people created a new movement called Black Lives Matter. It had receded somewhat during the nonstop chaos of Trump's presidency, but the killing of Floyd and others in early 2020 was a reminder that the violence continued, horrifying enough to start a popular rising.

The protests released the repressed energy of quarantine and freed people, especially young people, to be together in the streets for a just cause. Trump's name rarely came up. The target really was the police—and as the cops beat and gassed protesters, the rage grew incandescent. The protests seemed like an escape from what had become unbearable, into something else unbearable. It was that kind of year.

Thousands of doctors declared their solidarity and extended their indulgence. It had not been OK at all for Trump supporters to converge on state capitols in opposition to the lockdown, but it was OK for Black Lives Matter supporters to fill city streets in opposition to police brutality. The difference, according to the experts, was the cause. Racism actually endangered public health (but so did unemployment). A former director of the CDC, who had become an urgent voice for the lockdown, tweeted: "The threat to COVID control from protesting outside is tiny compared to the threat to COVID control created when governments act in ways that lose community trust. People can protest peacefully AND work together to stop COVID. Violence harms public health." To which a commenter replied: "This tweet makes me lose trust in our health authorities."

The experts had only the fragile legitimacy of science on their side, and they squandered it in one week and never got it all back. The mayor of New York lost more of his own dwindling authority when he announced that people who tested positive for the virus would not be asked about their participation in protests, meaning that their contacts could not be traced, though his science advisors insisted that such tracing was vital to track the spread. (Because the protests took place outdoors and many protesters wore masks, there was little increase in the following weeks. But that had not been the rationale of the experts.)

The anti-police protests and the anti-lockdown protests happened in the same period. Any overlap between the participants would not have filled a small lecture room. The anti-police protesters were mostly young, urban, progressive, and of all races. The anti-lockdown protesters were more likely middle-aged, small-town, conservative, and white. Politically, they were adversaries, if not enemies. In a couple of instances they fought each other. My sympathies were with the former much more than the latter.

But they had some things in common. The quarantine had stranded them all on lonely social media islands where they spent hours every day swamped with the remote like-minded in information that pulled them deeper into anger and self-justification. The pandemic sent everyone down one hole or another. Then they were driven out of isolation to protest what they saw as abusive state power. When they blocked traffic—a tactic that both groups used—they were asserting the supremacy of their rights over others'. "Whose streets? Our streets!" one group chanted, while the other waved signs that said "My Constitutional Rights Don't End

Where Your Fear Begins." (Eventually, the extreme right Proud Boys took up the left's "Whose streets? Our streets!") One group demanded justice and the other freedom, but protest was the first and maybe the only available recourse both groups found in our democratic politics.

Protest is one of the basic acts of citizenship, and in some contexts (for example, the civil rights movement) it's an expression of faith in the power of democratic institutions to bring change—the vigilance of a free press, the impartiality of the law, the conscience or self-interest of elected officials, the movability of public opinion. But the demonstrations of 2020 seemed different. They sounded more like howls in an institutional void—as if every other lever had become useless and protest was a last resort when self-government no longer worked. The protesters were railing against a society that wasn't cohesive enough to summon a response. Far from being oppressed by a powerful state, they were hammering on a hollow structure that was in danger of collapsing. That's why the George Floyd protests, as inspiring as they often were, did not fill me with hope. They seemed at once utopian and nihilistic.

After a few weeks the protests subsided. The most committed activists in places such as Minneapolis returned to the long work of changing how police departments treat Black citizens. Some local and state governments took up the issues of police accountability and criminal justice reform. Where the protests persisted, as in Portland, Oregon, they became increasingly violent and meaningless. But the spirit of the protests didn't go away. It left the streets and circulated into the culture more broadly—into universities, newspapers, arts organizations, publishing houses, nonprofits, corporations, Hollywood. The focus on police brutality expanded into something less tangible and far more ambitious, almost transhistorical. It was called anti-racism. For some Americans, especially educated white ones, the summer of 2020 became a season of white fragility, anti-Blackness, implicit bias, racial reckoning, allyship, and the "Fourth Founding" (after 1776, 1863, and 1965). This activism shifted the scene from blighted urban neighborhoods and prisons to human resources departments, anti-bias training sessions, and BIPOC reading lists. It was less interested in social reform than a revolution in consciousness.

The pandemic almost disappeared from mind as millions of white people experienced the kind of collective moral awakening that comes over Americans in different periods of our history. These awakenings can take on the contours of religious experience, a particularly American one—sin, denunciation, confession, atonement, redemption, heresy hunting, book burning, and the dream of paradise. Moral awakenings leap backward over the worldly philosophers of the eighteenth century, the secular and rationalist Founding Fathers, to our origins in the Puritan ancestors.

The passion and scale of the George Floyd protests gave some Americans the fervent belief that we were finally going to face our four centuries of crime and injustice. For conscious white people, this history remains saturated in collective shame and personal guilt, instantly revived by every viral video. The guilt comes in part from the knowledge of a permanent social class of Black misery that can be traced directly to the history. White Americans live with this class—accept it, in a sense—without wanting to see it too closely, like a chronic wound that never heals. Yet its existence is a constant indictment. The desire to be free of it is overpowering, but no one knows how to get there, the history is too deep, its effects too pervasive, from the achievement gap to the wealth gap to the COVID gap. Policy reforms don't come close. The only way out is to transform yourself. But how could anyone begin to do that?

So throughout the summer many white people turned, as educated Americans always do, to experts—not scientists, but activists and writers like Ibram X. Kendi, author of *How to Be an Anti-Racist*, a cross between an ideological tract and a self-help guide that became a huge bestseller, and Robin DiAngelo, author of *White Fragility*, who held encounter sessions that made white Americans confront their own complicity. The experts taught them that racism was not a matter of individual wrong, but a system in which everyone was enmeshed regardless of conduct or intent. For this reason the experts revived the term "white supremacy" and applied it to liberal-minded newspapers and foundations. White audiences sought out these painful lessons with the astonishing zeal and purpose that Americans muster for the most important national projects, like bomber production during World War II.

It was a strange time. Just about every company and organization with which I've ever had contact sent me emails describing the "work" they were doing to demonstrate their anti-racist bona fides. The CEO of the global megabank where I keep my savings sent out a letter to customers about "the progress we need to make to have a truly equal and just society." The refugee organization I support was suddenly denouncing "the cynical consequences of a nation that was built on the exploitation of Black people." Several hundred nonwhite theater artists posted an open letter called "We See You, White American Theater," declaring, "We have watched you un-challenge your white privilege, inviting us to traffic in the very racism and patriarchy that festers in our bodies, while we protest against it on your stages," and then sent follow-up letters to individual theater companies already engaged in earnest efforts to be inclusive—putting them on notice that they were being monitored. Elite private schools, such as St. Ann's and Dalton in New York, hired expensive trainers to eliminate bias and separated children into mandatory identity groups where they received anti-racist instruction. The young and angry learned how powerful moralizing can be, while the old and established confessed and hoped to keep their heads. A kind of cultural revolution was taking place, with all the excitement and terror such things convey.

It will be a long time before we know whether the protests of 2020 can come anywhere close to fulfilling their ambitions—not just to change policing and criminal justice in America, but also to bring full equality to Black Americans. Because structures of oppression are much too big for any one of us to budge, in a sense white people are, as usual, off the hook. Systemic criticism produces gestural politics. During the pandemic the San Francisco Board of Education took on the project of changing the names of Abraham Lincoln High School, Franklin D. Roosevelt Middle School, and dozens of other "problematically" named schools, while keeping isolated and demoralized children out of all schools, whatever their names. Mastheads and tables of contents changed, pictures and statues were taken down, glass ceilings shattered, but no one honestly expected to do much about the material conditions of misery. The summer of 2020 became an affair of, by, and for professionals. It led to few concrete ideas for helping disadvantaged Black people and a slogan ("defund the police") that created endless confusion and antagonism. Instead of a political agenda and strategy, it pursued a mystical vision that freezes us all in the ice of our own identity and makes ordinary communication with one another nearly impossible. In a memoir, Alicia Garza, who is credited with originating the term "Black lives matter," criticized the movement for being too insular, too intolerant, too ready to pursue trivial causes and avoid high-stakes politics. The protests were another part of the "social fact" of America—a country too incoherent to talk about its hardest problems in a way that begins to solve them.

The last major protest of the summer happened at the end of August, while the political parties were holding their conventions. It took place in the working-class city of Kenosha, in the important swing state of Wisconsin. Another police officer tried to kill another Black man who appeared to offer no immediate threat. Jacob Blake was shot seven times from behind; he somehow survived, paralyzed from the waist down. By the next night businesses in Kenosha were burning.

Two days after the shooting, and a few hours before an out-of-state seventeen-year-old killed two protesters with his AR-15, Blake's mother, Julia Jackson, drove through the charred streets of her hometown to appear before the cameras. She was a small churchgoing woman, and shock and grief were vivid on her face. But Julia Jackson gave the speech that Americans needed most to hear in 2020.

She began softly, almost inaudibly, but her own words seemed to give her strength, and finally a profound resonance. She said that her son would be "very unpleased" with the damage to his community. Speaking to Kenosha and the whole country, she said, "Do Jacob justice on this level and examine your hearts." She said that she had been praying for Jacob's healing, and, "even before this," for the healing of the country. "God has placed each and every one of us in this country because he wanted us to be here. Clearly you can see by now that I have beautiful brown skin. But take a look at your hand, and whatever shade it is, it is beautiful as well. How dare we hate what we are? We are human." She said, "Please, let's begin to pray for healing for our nation. We are the United States. Have we been united? Do you understand what's going to happen when we fall? Because a house that is against each other cannot stand." And she said, "Let's use our hearts, our love, and our intelligence to work together, to show the rest of the world how humans are supposed to treat each other. America *is* great when we behave great*ly*."

The weeks leading up to the November election were filled with dread. Vicious storms on the Gulf Coast, apocalyptic skies glowing orange at daybreak from wildfire smoke over baking California cities. Climate change was relentless, and so was the pandemic that seemed like a dry run of the world's ability to survive the larger event.

The election also inspired dread. If Trump won, we were finished—not just because of what he would be able to do, but because *we* had still wanted him to do it. "We must ourselves be its author and finisher," Lincoln said. If Trump lost, he would try to destroy the country rather than concede.

He told his followers that there would be massive ballot fraud and urged the tough ones, an "army for Trump," to swarm the polls and stop it. He squeezed one more justice onto the Supreme Court as a last-minute ace in the hole. Experts studied antique election laws to see how much trouble Trump could cause and discovered that there is nothing self-ratifying about the popular will. If democratic institutions—courts, state legislatures, and Congress—acquiesced, Trump could hang on to power as an unreelected dictator.

Democracy depends on belief in democracy—on an extraordinary leap of faith by ordinary people that their rulers will abide by the rules, that their votes will count, that their compatriots won't tear the country apart, that lies won't become truth. When the checks and balances have all given way, the last barrier to an authoritarian regime is public opinion. Even that might not be enough.

Not even a quarter of Americans expected the election to be free and fair. Three quarters expected violence to follow. Large minorities of both parties believed that violence would be justified if the vote didn't go their way. And yet three quarters of the country also believed that citizens, by their actions, could change society for the better. We were in the desperate position of clinging to something precious that we expected to betray us. For the election to succeed, we had to think and act as if it would succeed. We had to believe that democratic power still lay in our hands, or else we would have already surrendered it.

"Do you think there's going to be a civil war?"

"Not like the real Civil War. But it's going to be bad. Outbreaks here and there."

"I think it'll be a civil war."

In the days before the election, store owners boarded their windows, just as they'd done when the summer protests had turned violent. This never happened before. Millions of people were arming up. I wondered if I should do the same. My family strongly discouraged it. These conversations, entirely new and not entirely irrational, showed just how far the social contract had deteriorated.

But American democracy held. By the skin of its teeth, it held.

Trump charged incessantly that mail-in ballots in time of

plague would be "a complete fraud," trying to delegitimize them in advance—but the ballots poured in to post offices and drop boxes and polling centers across the country in record numbers. Then came the long lines on the first day of early voting—Americans by the millions, masked and standing apart, in Virginia and Texas and Georgia and New York, waiting in some places for hours, winding half a mile down city blocks and through suburban parks. The sight of those lines was something. Americans came out of isolation and depression, shuffling off their fatigue and gloom to vote. The sight said that we still had faith, abused as it was—democratic faith. That this one thing, the vote, belongs indisputably to us. If anything in America is sacred, this is, and at the end of the worst year of our lives we would not let it be taken or slip away. So we stood waiting one at a time, looking at a phone or staring at the sky, moving ahead a few feet, equal for a day.

At the start of the pandemic, supermarket cashiers and delivery drivers were suddenly heroes. At the end of the year the heroes were just as obscure: election officials, poll workers, vote counters. Despite the virus and the lies and the fears, the election of 2020 turned out to be the biggest and best run in American history. Voting systems were not hacked and rarely broke down. No one was still standing in line to vote at midnight. There was no violence on Election Day or the days after. My neighbors took down their signs even before the final result was announced.

Why did this one event go so well when everything else in the year had gone badly? There were technical reasons: intense preparation in the states, prepaid postage for absentee ballots, secure drop boxes, expanded early voting, requirements for backup paper ballots, improved cybersecurity and vote-counting machinery. There was also the civic virtue of individuals. When Trump tried to steal the election by having the result against him thrown out, nearly every prominent Republican politician said nothing, temporized about "the president's legal rights," or actively aided him in his assault on self-government. Senator Kelly Loeffler became one of Trump's most ardent helpers and pushed to get the votes of Georgians thrown out even while asking for the votes of those same Georgians in her run-off election in January—making sure that abuse of office characterized her entire year of public service. But most Republicans with actual responsibility—state election officials, federal judges, senior military officers—refused to nullify the popular will, even as they came under intense pressure and threats of violence, even as the nihilistic philosophy of "might makes right" tightened its grip on their party.

The higher reason, the *spiritual* reason, why democracy held was this: Americans still want it.

Before vacating his office, Trump left behind one last lie, bigger than all the others, a tale of the worst betrayal of democracy in American history: the presidential election had been stolen. Hundreds of Republican officials broke their oaths in order to advance the lie, and 70 percent of Republican voters believed it, and this belief brought the year to its apocalyptic end two weeks before Inauguration Day, on January 6, when a mob that Trump had summoned to Washington and incited to march on Congress just as it was voting to ratify his opponent's victory—20,000 neo-Confederate seditionists, QAnon conspiracists, white supremacists, and swag-wearing Trumpists, with their hats and flags and face paint, their sagging bellies and jeans—stormed the Capitol and searched for members of Congress to lynch, or else milled around taking selfies, while Trump watched with pleasure on TV, until our exhausted democracy mustered one last effort to save itself from destruction.

A stab-in-the-back narrative was buried in the minds of millions of Americans, where it will continue to burn, as imperishable as a carbon isotope, consuming whatever is left of their trust in democratic institutions and values. Long after the last COVID patient is buried or sent home alive, Trump's enduring legacy will be his 30,000 presidential lies. Superspread by social media and cable news, they will linger for years, poisoning the mental atmosphere like radioactive dust.

We are two countries—that was the real message of the 158 million votes. But we still have to live together. We're stuck with one another. That fact poses a supreme problem, one that will take even more urgency, intelligence, and cooperation than the remarkable achievement of a vaccine in less than a year. The election ended a terrible presidency, and the vaccine will end a terrible pandemic, and we are already forgetting the face in the mirror because that's how it is with painful things. But we shouldn't forget. I want to keep the image before you a little longer. We're still in the high-risk category.

FOUR AMERICAS

The year 2020 exposed our underlying conditions. But it did not explain why they exist, why we are divided, or how we can become a country again.

There are different accounts of what happened to bring us to this point:

1. The powerful few saw their chance and grabbed the spoils of capitalism for themselves.
2. Vast impersonal changes blew across the world, flattening old structures and leaving behind new groups of winners and losers.
3. One party descended into extremism and then nihilism, dragging half the country with it and making the whole country ungovernable.
4. The other party sliced up its half into groups, calculating that the sum of them would keep it in power.

5. America became more diverse, those long silent began to speak, and the traditional population sank into hateful opposition.

6. Bipartisan elites sold out their lower compatriots to a new global order.

7. The end of the Cold War took away our last national cause and set us fighting among ourselves in ever nastier skirmishes.

8. Americans went on a self-centered spree that continued for half a century while the common good withered away.

You might have your favorite version, or a different one altogether. I can't reject any of these outright. Warehouses of books are devoted to explaining how America became two countries. But if I were to put it in a single sentence, I would say: *Inequality undermined the common faith that Americans need to create a successful multi-everything democracy.* The postindustrial era has concentrated political and economic power in just a few hands and denied ordinary people control of their own lives. Overwhelmed by unfathomably large forces, Americans can no longer think and act as fellow citizens. We look for answers in private panaceas, fixed ideas, group identities, dreams of the future and the past, saviors of different types—everywhere but in ourselves. When none of these sets us free, we turn against one another.

But instead of analyzing trends and events and numbers,

I want to talk about what happened in terms of narratives. Nations, like individuals, tell stories in order to understand what they are, where they come from, and what they want to be. National narratives, like personal ones, are prone to sentimentality, grievance, pride, shame, self-blindness. There is never just one—they compete with one another and constantly change.

The most durable narratives are not the ones that stand up best to fact checking. They're the ones that address our deepest needs and desires. "Nobody knows what it would be like to try to be objective when attempting to decide what one's country really is, what its history really means, any more than when answering the question of who one really is oneself, what one's individual past really adds up to," the philosopher Richard Rorty wrote. "We raise questions about our individual or national identity as part of the process of deciding what we will do next, what we will try to become."

Put this way, these narratives sound almost like myths, which sound dangerous. We are supposed to be suspicious of myths and to go around puncturing them wherever we find them, ruthlessly replacing them with the truth. We know by now that democracy depends on a baseline of shared reality—when facts become fungible, we're lost. But just as no one can live a happy and productive life in nonstop self-criticism, nations require more than just facts—they need stories that convey a moral identity. The long gaze in the mirror has to end in self-respect or it will swallow us up.

For much of the twentieth century, the two parties had clear identities and told distinct stories. The Republicans spoke for those who wanted to get ahead, and the Democrats spoke for those who wanted a fair shake. The interests of business were on one side, workers on the other. Republicans emphasized individual enterprise, and Democrats emphasized social solidarity, eventually including Black people and abandoning the party's commitment to Jim Crow. But the two parties were arguing over the same recognizable country. The lineup held until the late sixties—still within living memory. In another couple of decades that country will disappear, as World War II is vanishing now.

In 1968, Norman Mailer described the political conventions of that apocalyptic year in his classic book *Miami and the Siege of Chicago*. In one scene, Richard Nixon greeted the Republican delegates in Miami Beach: "a parade of wives and children and men who owned hardware stores or were druggists, or first teller in the bank, proprietor of a haberdashery or principal of a small-town high school, local lawyer, retired doctor, widow on a tidy income, her minister and fellow-delegate, minor executives from minor corporations, men who owned their farms . . . out to pay homage to their own true candidate, the representative of their conservative orderly heart."

Imagine the Middle America of Mailer's delegate parade and compare it with the red heartland towns that make up Trump's base. It was an intact, smug, prosperous, white world—above all, it was "orderly." The inhabitants owned or worked in small businesses, sent their kids to decent public schools, attended mainline Protestant churches, and set aside money for a comfortable retirement. They got their news from the local paper, *Time* magazine, and Walter Cronkite. For entertainment they watched Lawrence Welk and *Gunsmoke*. They were going to vote for Nixon because they were Republicans, and because Nixon said that he would listen to "the voice of the great majority of Americans, the forgotten Americans, the non-shouters, the non-demonstrators." He promised to restore order, whose collapse was the core phenomenon of 1968, as the core phenomenon of 2020 was the failure of solidarity.

The Democratic gathering in Chicago was raw and disorderly. Mailer personified party regulars in the brutal proletarian jowls of Mayor Richard Daley, and in the flesh and smell of the stockyards next door to the convention hall. It was still primarily a working-class party. The delegates were labor leaders, ethnic ward heelers, southern pols, and liberal activists. This coalition was gathering for the last time. The Democratic Party's future was contested inside the hall and outside in the riotous streets.

The two parties were corrupt, undemocratic, and often bigoted, but they represented organized interests (unions, chambers of commerce) through traditional structures (the

Daley machine, the Republican county apparatus). They reflected a society that was less free than today, less tolerant, far less diverse, and with fewer choices, but with more economic equality, more shared prosperity, and more political cooperation. Republican liberals voted for Nixon, and Democratic conservatives voted for Hubert Humphrey. The major legislation of that year—fair housing, gun control— passed with bipartisan support. Americans were more uniform than we are in what they ate (tuna noodle casserole) and what they watched (*Bullitt*). Even their bodies looked more alike. They were more restrained than we are, more repressed—though restraint and repression were coming undone by 1968.

Chicago produced epic floor battles, street violence, and a nominee, Humphrey, who hadn't entered a single primary. At one point inside the convention hall, a U.S. senator at the podium denounced "Gestapo tactics in the streets of Chicago," and the city's mayor and convention host yelled back, "Fuck you, you Jew sonofabitch!" After 1968, the Democrats changed their nominating rules to make the party more open and democratic. They weakened the old bosses, brought the protesters inside, and strengthened participation by women, minorities, and single-issue activists. The class rhetoric of the New Deal sounded out of date to them; the issues it addressed appeared to have been solved by the wide prosperity of the postwar years. A different set of issues mattered to younger Democrats: the rights of disenfranchised groups, the environment, corruption, militarism.

The activists who had been cheated by the Daley machine in 1968 became the new bosses at the 1972 convention, which nominated George McGovern. That year, blue-collar, white, culturally conservative "Democrats for Nixon" helped re-elect the president in a landslide. These were the fore-runners of Reagan Democrats and, eventually, Trump Republicans. The changes of the early seventies marked a long-term Democratic shift in power from the white working class to the college-educated and minorities. It took several decades, but the two parties just about traded places. By the turn of the millennium, the Democrats were becoming the home of affluent professionals, while the Republicans were starting to sound like populist insurgents. We have to understand this exchange in order to grasp how we got to 2020.

For a long time the seventies seemed to have no plot—a shapeless, burnt-out interregnum between the high dramas of the sixties and the bright, hard edges of the Reagan era. A mishmash of musical styles and fads, a blur of failed presidents, a series of international fiascoes, a mood of cynicism and farce. I was a teenager, and I mainly remember longing to be somewhere else—either the future or the past would do. But now it's clear that all the important trends began in the seventies. It was the end of postwar, middle-class, bipartisan America.

The transformations of the 1970s broke up the old party alignment and with it the two relatively stable narratives of getting ahead and the fair shake. In their place four rival narratives have emerged, four accounts of America's moral identity. They have roots in history, but they are shaped by new social arrangements, new ways of living. They reflect schisms on both sides of the divide that has made us two countries. Over the past four decades the four narratives have taken turns exercising influence. They overlap, morph into one another, attract and repel one another. None can be understood apart from the others, because all four emerge from the same whole. Each diagnoses an aspect of the American unwinding that led to 2020. Taken together, they embody it.

1.

Call the first narrative *Free America*. In the past half century it's been the most politically powerful of the four. Free America draws on libertarian ideas, which it installs in the high-powered engine of consumer capitalism. The freedom it champions is very different from Tocqueville's art of self-government. It's personal freedom, without other people—the negative liberty of "Don't tread on me."

The conservative movement began to dominate the Republican Party in the 1970s, and then much of the country after 1980 with the presidency of Ronald Reagan. It uneasily wove together several strands of thought. One was traditionalist, a reaction against the utopian plans and moral chaos of modern secular civilization. The traditionalists were sin-fearing Protestants, orthodox Catholics, southern agrarians, would-be aristocrats, alienated individualists—dissidents in postwar America. They were appalled by the complacent vulgarity of the semi-educated masses. Their hero was Edmund Burke, and their enemy was John Dewey, the philosopher of American democracy. The traditionalists' elitism set them at odds with the main currents of American life—the only passage of American history that appealed to them was the quasi-feudal Old South—but their writings inspired the next generation of conservatives, including William F. Buckley, Jr., who introduced the first issue of *National Review* in 1955 with the famous vow that his new magazine "stands athwart history, yelling Stop, at a time when no one is inclined to do so."

Adjacent to the traditionalists were the anti-Communists. Many of them were former Marxists, like Whittaker Chambers and James Burnham, who carried their apocalyptic baggage with them when they moved from left to right. Politics for them was nothing less than the titanic struggle between good and evil, God and Man. The main target of their energy was the ameliorative creed of Eleanor Roosevelt and Arthur Schlesinger, Jr., good old liberalism, which they believed to be nothing but a paler communism—"the ideology of Western suicide," Burnham called it. The anti-Communists, like the traditionalists, were skeptics of democracy—its softness would doom it to destruction when World War III broke out. If these hectoring pessimists were the sum of modern conservatism, the movement would have died of joylessness by 1960.

The libertarians were different. They slipped more easily into the American stream. In their insistence on freedom they could claim to be descendants of Locke, Jefferson, and the classical liberal tradition. Some of them interpreted the Constitution as a libertarian document for individual and states rights under a limited federal government, not as a framework for the strengthened nation that the authors of *The Federalist Papers* thought they were creating. They had their favorite presidents, just not the usual ones. Grover Cleveland and Calvin Coolidge came in for high praise. Oddly, the most influential libertarians were Europeans, especially the Austrian economist Friedrich Hayek, whose polemic against collectivism, *The Road to Serfdom*, was a publishing sensation in America in 1944, during the most dramatic mobilization of economic resources by state power in history.

What distinguished libertarians from mainstream pro-business Republicans—Mailer's parade of delegates in Miami Beach—was their pure and uncompromising idea. What was it? Hayek: "Planning leads to dictatorship." The purpose of government is to secure individual rights, little else. One sip of social welfare and free government dies. A 1937 Supreme Court decision upholding parts of the New Deal was the beginning of American decline and fall. Libertarians were in rebellion against the midcentury, mixed-economy consensus. In spirit they were more radical than conservative. No compromise with social security administrators and central bankers! Death to Keynesian fiscal policy!

Despite or because of the purity of their idea, libertarians made common cause with segregationists, and racism informed their political movement from its beginnings in electoral politics. Their first hero, Senator Barry Goldwater, ran for president in 1964 as an insurgent against his own party establishment while opposing the civil rights bill on states-rights grounds. "Extremism in the defense of liberty is no vice!" he thundered to the Republican convention, before losing to Lyndon Johnson in a wipeout.

The first two strands of the conservative movement—elitist traditionalism and anti-communism—remained part of its DNA for half a century. Eventually the American people made clear their preference for taking pleasures where they wanted and the first faded, while the end of the Cold War rendered the second obsolete. But libertarianism stretches all the way to the present. The names Russell Kirk and James Burnham are mostly forgotten, but I've met Ayn Rand fanatics all over—among Silicon Valley venture capitalists, at the office of the Tampa Bay Tea Party, even on a road paving crew. Speaker of the House Paul Ryan (who read *Atlas Shrugged* in high school) brought her pitiless philosophy of egoism to policymaking on Capitol Hill. Libertarianism speaks to the American myth of the self-made man and the lonely pioneer on the plains. (Glorification of men is a recurring feature.) Americans would rather not think too much about society, and libertarians make it easy by leaving society out altogether. The passion for equality gives Americans the confidence of autodidacts who find their own path through the messy contingencies of life to Truth between the covers of a novel they discovered at age sixteen. Libertarianism, like Marxism, is a complete explanatory system. It appeals to super-smart engineers and others who never really grow up.

How did Free America become the dogma of the Republican Party and set the terms of American politics for years? Like any great political change, this one depended on ideas, an authentic connection with people's lives, and timing. Just as there would have been no Roosevelt revolution without the Great Depression, there would have been no Reagan revolution without the 1970s. Transformations don't happen when a blindingly original insight flashes across the sky. The arrival of Free America in power realized ideas that had originated in the period after World War II. In the face of institutional inertia, politics requires a long game. The economist Milton Friedman once wrote: "Only a crisis—actual or perceived—produces real change. When that crisis occurs, the actions that are taken depend on the ideas that are lying around. That, I believe, is our basic function: to develop alternatives to existing policies, to keep them alive and available until the politically impossible becomes politically inevitable." After years of high inflation with high unemployment, gas shortages, liberal cities in chaos, and epic government corruption and incompetence, by 1980 a large audience of Americans was ready to listen when Milton and Rose Friedman, in a book and ten-part public television series called *Free to Choose*, blamed the country's decline on business regulations and other government interventions in the market.

But it took the alchemy of that year's Republican nominee to transform the cold formula of tax cuts and deregulation into the warm vision of America as "the shining city on a hill"—land of the pilgrims, beacon to a desperate world. In Reagan's rhetoric, leveraged buyouts somehow rhymed with the spirit of New England town meetings. The oldest conflict in American politics is the one between individualism and centralism. Reagan changed the terms by inverting them: the descendants of Jefferson's yeoman farmers, with their desire for independence, became sturdy car-company executives and investment bankers yearning to breathe free of big government. The heirs of Hamilton's aristocratic financiers were unelected bureaucrats and uncaring regulators. Reagan made free-market economics sound like the ally of the ordinary American, and government the enemy. The hero of the new age was the risk-taking entrepreneur, latest in the lineage of American pioneers and inventors, Meriwether Lewises and Thomas Edisons who pursued their dreams in the face of hardship and neglect.

On election eve 1980, Reagan sat down by the fire and gave a televised closing speech in which he described his vision for the country. "Americans, who have always known that excessive bureaucracy is the enemy of excellence and compassion, want a change in public life—a change that makes government work *for* people," he said. "They seek a vision of a better America, a vision of society that frees the energy and ingenuity of our people while it extends compassion to the lonely, the desperate, and the forgotten. I believe that we can embark on a new era of reform in America and a new era of national renewal."

The speech ended with the shining city on a hill. Reagan made Free America sound like the Promised Land, a place where all were welcome to come pursue happiness. In 1980, the first year I cast a vote, I feared and hated Reagan. Listening to his words forty years later, I can hear their eloquence and understand their appeal, as long as I tune out many other things. Chief among them is Reagan's half-spoken message to white Americans: government only helps *those people*. He began his general election campaign at the Neshoba, Mississippi, county fair without mentioning the three civil rights workers who had been murdered nearby just sixteen years earlier. Legal segregation was barely dead when Free America, using the libertarian language of individualism and property rights, pushed the country into its long decline in public investment. The advantages for business were easy to see. As for ordinary people, the Republican Party reckoned that some white Americans would rather go without than share the full benefits of prosperity with their newly equal Black compatriots. Whitman, in *Leaves of Grass*, warned against this self-defeating prejudice: "Of Equality—As if it harm'd me, giving others the same chances and rights as myself—As if it were not indispensable to my own rights that others possessed the same."

Free America's hostility to government appealed to the new religious traditionalists. These weren't the alienated elites of an earlier time. They were white evangelicals who lived in midwestern towns and Sunbelt subdivisions, and their quarrel with government was mostly cultural, part of their larger quarrel with modern secular society: the local public school that was integrated by busing and banned prayer; the county commission that passed a gay rights ordinance; the federal government that gave their hard-earned tax dollars to welfare mothers in the depraved cities, replacing private charity with public coercion. The freedom they saw threatened was religious. These Christian foot soldiers of the revolution were not at all libertarians—they wanted morality brought into every corner of public life—but the narrative of Free America gave them a common enemy. Reagan attached their agenda to the program of the business class, but the Christians always brought up the rear and never achieved their goals, because Free America was OK with modern secular society as long as government got out of the way.

The majority of Americans who elected Reagan president did not vote for the destruction of the blue-collar workforce, or the rise of a new plutocracy, or legislation rigged in favor of organized money. They weren't told that Free America would break their unions and starve their social programs, or that it would change antitrust policy to bring a new age of monopoly, concentrating financial power and strangling competition, making Walmart, Citigroup, Google, and Amazon the J. P. Morgan and Standard Oil of a second Gilded Age. They had never heard of Charles and David Koch—heirs to a family oil business, libertarian billionaires, who would pour money into the lobbies and propaganda machines and political campaigns of Free America on behalf of corporate power and fossil fuels. Freedom sealed a deal between elected officials and business executives: campaign contributions in exchange for tax cuts and corporate welfare. The numerous scandals of the 1980s exposed the crony capitalism that lay at the heart of Free America.

The shining city on a hill was supposed to replace remote big government with a community of energetic and compassionate citizens, all engaged in a project of national renewal. But nothing held the city together. It was hollow at the center, a collection of individuals all wanting more. Free America measured civic health by gross domestic product. It saw Americans as entrepreneurs, employees, investors, taxpayers, and consumers—everything but citizens.

Free America's foreign policy was an extension of its view of American society, with godless communism in place of soulless bureaucracy, and the city on a hill reaching out to the entire free world and beyond. The narrative was imbued with American exceptionalism: the idea that our birth in freedom makes America different from and superior to all other countries, that providence and history have given us a unique mission to bring freedom to the world. Free America was intensely nationalistic—the 1984 Summer Olympics in Los Angeles were an orgy of flag waving, "USA!" chanting, and medal hoarding—but not in an insular way. Just as consumer capitalism became synonymous with individual freedom, U.S. power became a global crusade for democracy.

Free America placed uncritical faith in American ideals and American arms, on which it spent heavily. "We must be staunch in our conviction that freedom is not the sole prerogative of a lucky few, but the inalienable and universal right of all human beings," Reagan said to the British parliament in 1982. Paraphrasing Churchill during World War II, he asked, "What kind of people do we think we are?" and answered: "Free people, worthy of freedom and determined not only to remain so but to help others gain their freedom as well."

At its best, this faith gave support and inspiration to dissidents behind the Iron Curtain. At its worst, it fueled dirty proxy wars in poor countries under Communist rule. These wars, asking no sacrifices of Americans except a willingness to use violence against weak adversaries, reflected the emptiness and corruption beneath the glittering generalities of Free America.

In the Declaration of Independence, freedom comes right after equality. For Reagan and the narrative of Free America, it meant freedom *from* government and the bureaucrats. It meant the freedom to run a business without regulation, to pay workers whatever wage the market would bear, to break a union, to pass all your wealth on to your children, to buy out an ailing company with debt and strip it for assets, to own seven houses, or to go homeless. But a freedom that gets rid of all obstructions is impoverished, and it degrades people.

Real freedom is closer to the opposite of breaking loose.

It means having to grow up. Here's another version of freedom, from John Dewey: "The attainment of freedom conceived as power to act in accord with choice depends upon positive and constructive changes in social arrangements." Freedom is a power to do something. To do what? To act as you choose. But this power depends on your ability to change social conditions that advantage some people over others. If you try to exercise freedom in the vacuum of yourself, you will always be at the mercy of others with more power.

This is why freedom isn't free. It brings you out of shallow isolation into the deeper responsibilities of self-government. Freedom is the ability to participate fully in political and economic life. The obstructions that need to be removed are the ones that block this ability. Some are outside you, in institutions and social conditions. Others are embedded in your character and get in the way of governing yourself, thinking for yourself, and even knowing what is true. These obstructions crush the individuality that freedom lovers cherish and make them conformist, submissive, all shouting the same thing—easy marks for a demagogue. *Here, take my freedom for me, I can't bear it.*

Reagan cared more about the functions of self-government than his most ideological supporters. He knew how to persuade and when to compromise. But after he was gone, and the Soviet Union not long after him, Free America lost the narrative thread. Without Reagan's smile and the Cold War's clarity, its vision grew darker and more extreme. Its spirit

became flesh in the person of Newt Gingrich, the most influential politician of the past half century. There was nothing conservative about Gingrich. He came to Congress not
to work within the institution or even to change it, but to
tear it down in order to seize power. With the Gingrich
revolution, the term "government shutdown" entered the
lexicon and politics became a forever war (he liked to quote
Mao's definition of politics as "war without blood"). His tactics turned the goal of limited and efficient government into
the destruction of government. Without a positive vision,
his party used power to hold on to power and fatten corporate allies. Corruption—financial, political, intellectual,
moral—set in like dry rot in a hollow log.

There had been a mandarin air to the earlier conservatives, a revulsion toward mass society and the rebellious
ethos of the sixties. Irving Kristol, the father of neocon-
servatism, made the crucial point that democratic repub-
lics have to link "popular government to a fair measure
of self-government (i.e., self-discipline) on the part of the
individual citizen. The departure from these principles has
taken the form of a 'liberation' of personal and collective
selves—a freeing of self-interests, personal aspirations, private fantasies." That was in 1972, when indiscipline was
youthful and left-wing. In the eighties and nineties, conservatives made common cause with aggressive populists of talk
radio and Fox News who flouted the traditional virtues of
reason, prudence, and self-control. The boring Republican
Party of Mailer's druggists and retired doctors was suddenly

infused with a powerful energy. In 1985 Kristol amended his view: "This new populism is no kind of blind rebellion against good constitutional government. It is rather an effort to bring our governing elites to their senses. That is why so many people—and I include myself—who would ordinarily worry about a populist upsurge find themselves so sympathetic to this new populism." Kristol and other intellectuals were OK with the right kind of populists.

But the new populism did not have a "conservative orderly heart." It mocked self-government—both the political and the personal kind. It was riven with destructive impulses. It fed on rage and celebrity culture. The quality of Free America's leaders steadily deteriorated—falling from Reagan to Gingrich to Ted Cruz, from William F. Buckley to Ann Coulter to Sean Hannity—with no bottom.

The narrative of Free America remained as inflexible as any ideology: tax cuts and deregulation = freedom and prosperity. Decade after decade you encountered its mantra, like the rituals of a cargo cult, on the website of the Cato Institute, the editorial page of *The Wall Street Journal*, broadcasts of *The Rush Limbaugh Show*, and the platform of the Republican Party. The facts said otherwise. Wages for most Americans rose only when taxes on the rich went up under Bill Clinton. The years from Reagan onward were a general period of wage stagnation and inequality, of huge fortunes accumulating at the top and large parts of the country losing industries and Main Streets. What did freedom mean to a laid-off machinist whose company was bought out by private equity investors, stripped for assets, and his job sent across the border, while he found work as a security guard at Home Depot for half the pay?

While the sunny narrative of Free America shone on, its policies eroded the way of life of many of its adherents. The disappearance of secure employment and small businesses destroyed the fabric of communities. The civic associations that Tocqueville identified as the antidote to individualism died with the jobs. When towns lost their Main Street drugstores and restaurants to Walgreens and Wendy's in the big-box mall out on the highway, they also lost their Rotary Club and newspaper—the local institutions of self-government. This hollowing out exposed them to an epidemic of aloneness, physical and psychological. Middle-class people lived on debt to avoid falling into poverty, but they fell anyway. Isolation bred distrust in the old sources of authority—school, church, union, company, media.

Government, which did so little for ordinary Americans, was still the enemy, along with "governing elites." But for the sinking working class, freedom lost whatever economic meaning it once had. It was a matter of personal dignity, *identity*. It began to see trespassers everywhere and became the slogan of a defiant and armed loneliness: *Get the fuck off my property. Take this mask and shove it.* It was the threatening image of a coiled rattlesnake: "Don't tread on me." It achieved its ultimate expression on the last day of 2020, in all those yellow Gadsden flags waving around the Capitol—a mob of freedom-loving Americans taking back their constitutional rights by shitting on the floors of Congress and hunting down elected representatives to kidnap and kill. That was their freedom in its pure and reduced form.

A character in Jonathan Franzen's 2010 novel *Freedom* puts it this way: "If you don't have money, you cling to your freedoms all the more angrily. Even if smoking kills you, even if you can't afford to feed your kids, even if your kids are getting shot down by maniacs with assault rifles. You may be poor, but the one thing nobody can take away from you is the freedom to fuck up your life." The character is almost paraphrasing Barack Obama's notorious statement at a San Francisco fundraiser about the way white working-class Americans "cling to guns or religion or antipathy toward people who aren't like them, or anti-immigrant sentiment or anti-trade sentiment, as a way to explain their frustrations." The thought wasn't mistaken, but the condescension was self-incriminating. It showed why Democrats couldn't fathom that people might "vote against their interests." Guns and religion *were* the authentic interest of millions of Americans. Trade and immigration *had* left some of them worse off. And if the Democratic Party wasn't on their side—if government failed to improve their lives—why not vote for the party that at least took them seriously?

Free America always had an insurgent mindset, breaking institutions down, not building them up. Irresponsibility was coded into its leadership. Rather than finding new policies to repair the social fabric, Republicans mobilized anger and despair while offering up scapegoats. The party thought it could control these dark energies on its quest for more power, but instead they would consume it.

"Excessive bureaucracy" had helped bring on American decline in the 1970s, but by the first decade of the new century the problems were new ones. Free America's narrative was out of date.

A new narrative was taking its place. I first became aware of it during the 2008 presidential campaign, in a desolate Appalachian coal town called Glouster, Ohio, not far from the West Virginia border. No one eating breakfast at Bonnie's Home Cooking had much interest in either of the presidential candidates, Obama or John McCain, but several women were excited about McCain's vice presidential pick, the governor of Alaska, Sarah Palin. "She'd fit right in with us," Greta Jennice said. "We should invite her over." I heard the same enthusiasm from others in the area. Palin was a working-class hockey mom who strutted onstage at campaign events to Gretchen Wilson's anthem "Redneck Woman." The women at Bonnie's weren't bothered at all by Palin's obvious ignorance. They weren't interested in her policy views or professional experience. What drew them to her was identity. She was the future.

2.

The new knowledge economy created a new class of Americans: men and women with college degrees (at the very least), skilled with symbols and numbers, salaried professionals in information technology, scientific research, design, management consulting, the upper civil service, financial analysis, medicine, law, journalism, the arts, higher education. They go to college with one another, intermarry, gravitate to desirable neighborhoods in large metropolitan areas, and do all they can to pass on their advantages to their children. Their success depends on brainpower, not the exploitation of natural resources or accumulation of capital. They are not 1 percenters—those are mainly executives and investors—but they dominate the top 10 percent of American incomes, with outsized economic and cultural influence. When I was growing up, educated professionals belonged to the middle class or, more precisely, the upper middle class. A higher degree has become such a bright line between winning and losing that the more successful in the new generation are an upper class.

They're at ease in the world that modernity created. They were early adopters of things that make the surface of contemporary life agreeable: HBO, Lipitor, Mileage Plus Platinum, the MacBook Pro, organic grass-fed beef, cold-brewed coffee, Amazon Prime. They welcome novelty and relish diversity. They believe that the transnational flow of human beings, information, goods, and capital ultimately benefits most if not all people around the world. You have a hard time telling what part of the country they come from, because they speak in the same public radio accents and their local identities are submerged in the homogenizing culture of top universities and elite professions. Their manners are softer than those of their ancestors, but they're fiercely driven. They believe in credentials and expertise—not just as tools for success, but as qualifications for class entry. Their watchwords are "ideas," "innovation," and "smart." They're not nationalistic—the very opposite—but they have a national narrative. Call it *Smart America.*

The cosmopolitan outlook of Smart America overlaps in some areas with the libertarian views of Free America. Each embraces capitalism and the principle of meritocracy: the belief that your talent and effort should determine your reward. In the narrative of Smart America, meritocracy stands alongside democracy as the twin pillars of the American system. Both are subject to criticism and improvement, and this is where Smart America differs from Free America. Libertarians believe that the market alone determines value, and that any attempt to tip the scales will upset its laws while endangering freedom. To the meritocrats of Smart America, some interventions are necessary for everyone to have an equal chance to move up. The long history of racial injustice demands remedies in affirmative action, diversity hiring, and maybe even reparations. The poor need a social safety net and a living wage; poor children deserve higher spending on education and health care. Workers dislocated by trade agreements, automation, and other blows of the global economy should be retrained for new kinds of jobs.

But there's a limit to how much government the meritocrats will accept. Social liberalism comes easier to them than redistribution, especially as they accumulate wealth like the bigger capitalists and look to their 401(k)s and other investments for long-term security. As for unions, they hardly exist in Smart America. They're instruments of class solidarity, not individual advancement, and the individual is the unit of worth in Smart America as in Free America. It's impossible to imagine a successful life that doesn't involve rising from a good university into a good career. The ideal of equality still exists, but firmly within the system of meritocracy, which distributes not just economic rewards but something at least as valuable: social status.

The word "meritocracy" has been around since the late 1950s, when a British sociologist named Michael Young published *The Rise of the Meritocracy*. He meant this new word as a warning: modern societies would learn how to measure intelligence in children so exactly that they would be stratified in schools and jobs according to their natural ability. In Young's satirical fantasy this new form of inequality would be so rigid and oppressive that it would end in violent rebellion.

But the word lost its original dystopian meaning. When meritocracy was young in this country, it almost lived up to its name. In the decades after World War II, the G.I. Bill, the advent of standardized tests, the civil rights movement, and the opening of top universities to minorities, women, and children of the middle and working classes all combined to offer a path upward that probably came as close to truly equal opportunity as America has ever seen.

After the 1970s, meritocracy began to look more and more like Michael Young's dark satire. A system intended to give each new generation an equal chance to rise created a new hereditary class structure. Educated professionals pass on their money, connections, ambitions, and work ethic to their children, while less educated families fall further behind, with diminishing chances of seeing their children move up. By kindergarten, upper-class children are already a full two years ahead of their lower-class counterparts, and the achievement gap is almost unbridgeable. After seven decades of meritocracy, it's as unlikely for a lower-class child to be admitted to a top Ivy League university as it was in 1954. The country that always modeled social mobility for the rest of the world has become more class-ridden than recent aristocracies like Austria and Japan.

This hierarchy slowly hardened over the decades without drawing much notice. It's based on education and merit, and education and merit are good things, so who would question it? And there are plenty of exceptions to disguise the deeper injustice, children who rose from modest backgrounds to the heights of society. Bill Clinton, for example (who talked about "people who work hard and play by the rules"), Hillary Clinton (who liked the phrase "God-given talents"), and Barack Obama ("We need every single one of you to develop your talents, skills, and intellect")—all products of the meritocracy. *Of course* individuals should be rewarded according to their ability. What's the alternative? Either collectivization or aristocracy. Either everyone gets the same grades and salaries regardless of achievement, which is unjust and horribly mediocre, or else everyone has to live out the life into which they're born, which is unjust and horribly regressive. Meritocracy seems like the one system that answers the American passion for equality. If the opportunities are truly equal, the results will be fair.

But it's this idea of fairness that accounts for meritocracy's cruelty. If you don't make the cut, you have no one and nothing to blame but yourself. Those who make it can feel morally pleased with themselves—their talents, discipline, good choices—and even a grim kind of satisfaction when they run across someone who hasn't made it. Not "There but for the grace of God go I," not even "Life is unfair," but "You should have been more like me." During the Great Recession I met an out-of-work welder who had dropped out of high school in his senior year. He attributed all his subsequent troubles—unemployment, poverty, poor health, children with blighted prospects—to this decision, which had been his alone. He had learned the hard lesson of meritocracy.

Politically, Smart America came to be associated with the Democratic Party. This was never inevitable. If the party had refused to accept the closing of factories in the 1970s and '80s as a natural disaster, if it had become the voice of the millions of workers displaced by deindustrialization and struggling in the growing service economy, it might have remained the multi-ethnic working-class party that it had been since the 1930s. It's true that the white South abandoned the Democratic Party after the civil rights revolution, but race alone doesn't explain the epochal half-century shift of the white working class. West Virginia, almost all white, was a Democratic state until 2000 (since that year it's voted Republican in every presidential election). If you look at county-by-county national electoral maps, 2000 is the year when vast rural areas turned decisively and permanently red. Something more than just the Democrats' principled embrace of the Black freedom movement and other struggles for equality caused the shift.

After the McGovern convention in 1972, the Democratic Party became the home of educated professionals, racial minorities, and the shrinking unionized working class. The more the party identified with the winners of the new economy, the easier it became for the Republican Party to pull away white workers by appealing to cultural values. In the 1980s Gary Hart (who had labored on the Kansas railroads as a boy) became the leader of the tech-minded "Atari Democrats." In the early 1990s Bill Clinton (from a dirt-poor Arkansas watermelon patch called Hope) used his chairmanship of the centrist Democratic Leadership Council as a launchpad for the presidency. Even though Clinton sounded like an Ozark populist, old-fashioned class politics was foreign to him. Bill and Hillary Clinton were policy wonks who mashed together idealism with business-friendly ideas for economic growth. Instead of speaking for the working class, the Clintons spoke about equipping workers to rise into the professional class through education and training.

Their assumption was that all Americans could do what they did and be like them.

The narrative of Free America shaped the parameters of acceptable thinking for Smart America. Free trade, deregulation, economic concentration, and balanced budgets became the policy of the Democratic Party. Culturally it was cosmopolitan, embracing multiculturalism at home and welcoming an increasingly globalized world. Its donor class on Wall Street and in Silicon Valley bankrolled Democratic campaigns and was rewarded with dominant influence in Washington. None of this appealed to the party's old base. Culture usually beats class in American politics, and a tolerant, inclusive Democratic Party would have needed better policies and politicians to hold on to culturally conservative voters. As things played out, the 1990s, a triumphalist decade for the party and the country, were the years when the Democrats embraced Smart America and lost the white working class.

Lawrence Summers, a senior official in Clinton's Treasury department who became secretary in 1999, later described to me all the trips he took to review anti-poverty programs in Africa, Latin America, and the largest U.S. cities. "I don't think I ever went to Akron, or Flint, or Toledo, or Youngstown," he admitted. The problems of displaced workers in the Rust Belt, including white workers, "weren't heavily on our radar screen, and they were mad that their problems weren't." It's easy to imagine how those white workers never made the radar screen in Washington. They went against type. They weren't the classic downtrodden and oppressed. They were in some ways unattractive, with their provincial views and hypermasculine ways—an embarrassment to a political class at home in the fluid world of transnational corporations, blended identities, and multicultural education.

In 1999 Thomas Friedman published *The Lexus and the Olive Tree: Understanding Globalization*. It was *Das Kapital* for Smart America. In Friedman's account, globalization is the organizing system of the post–Cold War era, but, unlike the Cold War, it is the result of technological advances and blind economic forces, not government policies. Rejecting globalization is like rejecting the sunrise. The descriptions sounded neutral, but they kept slipping into admiration and exhortation. The new system is not only inevitable but the best of all possible worlds, and the train is about to leave the station—get on board *right away* or you'll be left behind or flattened. Only the shortsighted, the stupid, the coddled, and the unprepared would try to stop globalization. Its heroes are entrepreneurs, financiers, and technologists, hopping airports between New York, San Francisco, London, Hong Kong. The book became essential reading for the meritocrats it flattered.

The turn of the millennium was the high-water mark of Smart America. Clinton's speeches became euphoric—"We are fortunate to be alive at this moment in history," he said in his final State of the Union message. The new economy had replaced "outmoded ideologies" with dazzling technologies. The business cycle had practically been abolished, along with class conflict. The answer to all problems of social class was education. Clinton's wish list to Congress that year included more money for Internet access in schools and college-test-prep courses for poor kids. In April 2000 Clinton hosted a celebration called the White House Conference on the New Economy. Bill Gates sat on a panel with Amartya Sen, earnest purpose mingled with self-congratulation, virtue and success high-fived—the distinctive atmosphere of Smart America. At one point Clinton informed the participants that Congress was about to pass a bill for permanent trade relations with China, which would make both countries more prosperous and China more free. "I believe the computer and the Internet give us a chance to move more people out of poverty more quickly than at any time in all of human history," he exulted.

You can almost date the election of Donald Trump to that moment.

The winners in Smart America have withdrawn from the national life of their fellow Americans. Christopher Lasch, writing in the early 1990s when this withdrawal was young, called it "the revolt of the elites." Between meritocracy and democracy, it's the first that dominates their waking hours, commands their unthinking devotion, and drives them, like orthodox followers of an exacting faith, to extraordinary, even absurd feats of exertion. Smart Americans spend inordinate amounts of time working (even in bed), researching their children's schools and planning their activities, shopping for the right kind of food, learning to make sushi or play the mandolin, staying in shape, and following the news. Even the last is a private activity. It doesn't bring them in contact with fellow citizens outside their way of life. School, the most universal and influential of our democratic institutions, increasingly walls them off from those below. The working class is terra incognita.

There is nothing new in the pursuit of success. The Smart American is a descendant of the self-made man of the early nineteenth century, who raised the work ethic to the highest personal virtue, and the urban Progressive of the early twentieth, who revered expertise. But there's a difference: the path is narrower, it leads to institutions with high walls, and the gate is harder to open.

Smart Americans have withdrawn—but not into private bliss. Meritocracy is a harsh master, and it doesn't make its followers happy. They live with a constant background hum of anxiety, a feeling of having arrived a few minutes late with all the seats taken. The most important event in the life cycle of a family—the frenzied competition for admission into a top-twenty *U.S. News*–rated college—is filled with fear and self-reproach. Under the watchful eye of their parents, children devote exhausting amounts of energy to hollow, inauthentic pursuits like unwanted extracurricular activities and carefully constructed personal essays that can navigate the straits between boasting and humility. The ordeal ends in a brief letter that brings either excessive pride (*Congratulations, you're one of the elect!*) or warrantless disappointment (*We're sure you'll find happiness somewhere*), delivering the final verdict on a whole life. What's worse, the verdict is completely just, because meritocracy chooses winners and losers based on ability. The goal of all this effort is a higher education that offers questionable learning, dubious fulfillment, likely indebtedness, but certain status.

A rite endowed with so much importance and involving so little of real value resembles the brittle decadence of an aristocracy that's reached the stage when people begin to lose faith that it's the natural order of things. In our case, a system intended to expand equality has become an enforcer of inequality. Americans are now meritocrats by birth. They know this and, because it violates their fundamental beliefs, they go to a lot of trouble not to know it.

In the class structure of Smart America, meritocrats occupy an important level. Above them sit the always-getting-richer very rich, whom they regard with loathing and envy, and at whom they direct a continuous barrage of critical fire. Most of the books and columns and gossip aimed at the 1 percent come from people just a few percentage points below, implying that the high salaries of elite professionals are legitimately earned, while the capital windfalls of business executives and investors are crooked. Below the meritocrats are the vast middle and working classes, some with college degrees and some without—skilled tradespeople, government clerks, schoolteachers—all in constant peril of being right-sized or automated into the ranks of the working poor, where supermarket cashiers and warehouse workers toil for low wages. The hazardous lives of those below are a source of quiet self-congratulation for meritocrats, but smugness barely holds down a deeper feeling, which is fear. The fall is steep, and when parents on the fortunate ledge of this chasm look down, vertigo stuns them. Far below, they see a dim world of processed food, obesity, divorce, addiction, online-education scams, stagnant wages, rising morbidity rates—and they pledge to do whatever they can to keep their children from falling. They'll stay married, cook organic family dinners, read aloud at bedtime every night, take out a crushing mortgage on a house in a highly rated school district, pay for music teachers and test-prep tutors, and donate repeatedly to overendowed alumni funds.

It's common now, in places like southeastern Ohio and Southside Virginia and central Pennsylvania, to hear that the middle class no longer exists. A woman in her sixties in Tampa, a retired municipal employee who had made and then lost money in real estate, described herself to me as a member of "the formerly middle class." She meant that she no longer lived with any security. Her term could apply to a non-union electrician making $52,000 a year and a home health aide making $12 an hour. The first still belongs financially to the middle class, while the second is working class—in fact, working poor. What they share is a high school diploma and a precarious prospect. Neither of them can look with confidence on their future, less still on their children's. The dream of leaving their children better educated and better off has lost its conviction, and therefore its inspiration. They can't possibly attain the shiny, well-ordered lives they see in the houses of elite professionals for whom they work. The espresso maker on the quartz countertop, the art hanging on the living room walls, the shelves of books lining the children's bedrooms—glimpses of a foreign culture. What professionals actually do to earn the large incomes that pay for their nice things is a mystery. All those hours spent sitting at a computer screen—do they contribute something to society, to the family of an electrician or a home health aide (whose contributions are obvious)? What's the point of merit that exists only to protect privilege? What if their expensive educations and lucrative careers are designing an economy that keeps others out while creating a future in which only Americans like them continue to rise? Then Smart America is another rigged system.

So these two classes, rising professionals and sinking workers, which a couple of generations ago were close in incomes and not so far apart in mores, no longer believe they belong to the same country. But they can't escape each other, and their coexistence in Smart America breeds condescension, resentment, and shame. Daniel Markovits, a Yale law professor and author of *The Meritocracy Trap*, describes the relationship as "a close but hostile embrace. Meritocratic inequality inspires the hostility, entwining the classes in misunderstandings, friction, discord, and even open warfare."

As a national narrative, Smart America has a tenuous sense of the nation. It's a cosmopolitan narrative, so where does that leave your country? Smart America never adopted the normal anti-Americanism of the post-sixties left. It doesn't *hate* America, which has been so good to the meritocrats. Smart Americans believe in institutions, and they support American leadership of military alliances and international organizations. In some cases they've endorsed smart wars fought with smart bombs, especially with a humanitarian purpose. They were divided by Iraq. "I am not opposed to all wars," Barack Obama said at an antiwar rally in Chicago in 2002. "I'm opposed to dumb wars."

But Smart Americans are uneasy with patriotism. It's an unpleasant relic of a more primitive time, like cigarette smoke or dog racing. It wakes up emotions that can have ugly consequences, from sports fans chanting "USA! USA!" all the way to the hypernationalism of the post-9/11 years. The shining city on a hill is heavily armed and dangerous. Better let patriotism sleep, or rather, better leave it for dead. The winners in Smart America—connected by airplane, Internet, and investments to the rest of the globe—have lost the capacity and the need for a national identity, which is why they can't grasp its importance for others. Their passionate loyalty, the one that gives them a particular identity, goes to their family. The rest is diversity and efficiency, heirloom tomatoes and self-driving cars. They don't see the point of patriotism.

In 2004 the Harvard political scientist Samuel Huntington published his last book, *Who Are We?* It was a cry of alarm about the demise of American identity under globalization. *The New Yorker* gave it a withering review for raising a panic about something obsolete: "If the world is becoming more porous, more transnational, more tuned to the same economic, social, and informational frequency—if the globe is more global, which means more Americanized—then the need for national cultural homogeneity is lesser, not greater. The stronger societies will be the more cosmopolitan ones." It would be hard to find a better summary of the narrative of Smart America. To be global is to be Americanized, and to be American is to be globalized. This victory is all the patriotism that meritocrats need.

Patriotism can be turned to good or ill purposes, but in most people it never dies. It's a persistent attachment, like loyalty to your family, a source of meaning and together-ness, strongest when it's hardly conscious. Like family loy-alty, national loyalty doesn't require you to reject or abuse others, but it's an attachment to what makes your country *yours*, distinct from the rest, even when you can't stand it, even when it breaks your heart. This feeling can't be wished out of existence. And because people still live their lives in an actual place, and the nation is the largest place with which they can identify—world citizenship is too abstract to be meaningful—patriotic feeling has to be tapped if you want to achieve anything big. If your goal is to slow climate change, or reverse inequality, or stop racism, or rebuild de-mocracy, you will need the national solidarity that comes from patriotism.

That's one problem with the narrative of Smart Amer-ica. The other problem is that abandoning patriotism to other narratives guarantees that the worst of them will claim it.

3.

In the fall of 2008, Sarah Palin spoke at a fundraiser in Greensboro, North Carolina. Candidates reserve the truth for their donors, using the direct language they avoid with the press and public (Obama: "cling to guns and religion"; Romney: "the 47 percent"; Clinton: "basket of deplorables"), and Palin felt free to speak openly. "We believe that the best of America is in these small towns that we get to visit," she said, "and in these wonderful little pockets of what I call the real America, being here with all of you hardworking, very patriotic, pro-America areas of this great nation. Those who are running our factories and teaching our kids and growing our food and are fighting our wars for us."

What made Palin alien to people in Smart America attracted thousands to stand in line for hours at her rallies in *Real America*: her vernacular ("you betcha," "drill, baby, drill"), her charismatic Christianity, her rimless glasses, the four colleges she attended, her five children's names (Track, Bristol, Willow, Piper, Trig), her Down syndrome baby, her pregnant unwed teenage daughter, her husband's commercial fishing business, her hunting poses. She was working class to her boots. Plenty of politicians come from the working class—Palin never left it.

She went after Obama with particular venom. Her animus was fueled by his suspect origins, radical associates, and redistributionist views, but the worst offense was his galling mix of class and race. Obama was a Black professional who had gone to the best schools, knew so much more than Palin, and was too cerebral and classy to get in the mud pit with her.

Palin disintegrated during the campaign. Her miserable performance under basic questioning disqualified her for Americans with open minds on the subject. Her Republican handlers tried to hide her and later disowned her. In 2008 the country was still too rational for a candidate like Palin. After losing, she quit being governor of Alaska, which no longer interested her, and started a new career as a reality-TV personality, Tea Party star, and autographed merchandise saleswoman. Palin kept looking for a second act that never came. She suffered the pathetic fate of being a celebrity ahead of her time. For with her candidacy something new came into our national life that was also traditional. She was a western populist who embodied white identity politics. In her proud ignorance, unrestrained narcissism, and contempt for the "establishment," she was John the Baptist to the coming of Trump.

Real America is a very old place. The idea that the authentic heart of democracy beats hardest in common people who work with their hands goes back to the eighteenth century. It was embryonic in the founding creed of equality. "State a moral case to a ploughman and a professor," Jefferson wrote in 1787. "The former will decide it as well, and often better than the latter, because he has not been led astray by artificial rules." Moral equality was the basis for political equality. As the new republic became a more egalitarian society in the first decades of the nineteenth century, the democratic creed turned openly populist. Andrew Jackson came to power and governed as champion of "the humble members of society— the farmers, mechanics, and laborers," the Real Americans of that age. The Democratic Party dominated elections by pinning the charge of aristocratic elitism on the Federalists, and then the Whigs, who learned that they had to campaign on log cabins and hard cider to compete.

The triumph of popular democracy brought an anti-intellectual bias to American politics that never entirely disappeared. Self-government didn't require any special learning, just the native wisdom of the people. "Even in its earliest days," Richard Hofstadter wrote, "the egalitarian impulse in America was linked with a distrust for what in its germinal form may be called political specialization and in its later forms expertise." Hostility to aristocracy widened into a general suspicion of educated sophisticates. The more learned citizens were actually *less* fit to lead; the best politicians came from the ordinary people and stayed true to them. Making money didn't violate the spirit of equality— Americans should enjoy "the fruits of superior industry, economy, and virtue," Jackson said, without the benefit of "artificial distinctions"—but an air of superior knowledge did, especially when it cloaked special privileges.

There was nothing new about the overwhelmingly white crowds that lined up to hear Palin speak. Real America has always been a country of white people. Jackson himself was a slaver and an Indian killer, and his "farmers, mechanics, and laborers" were the all-white forebears of William Jennings Bryan's "producing masses," Huey Long's "little man," George Wallace's "rednecks," Patrick Buchanan's "pitchfork brigade," and Palin's "hardworking patriots." The political positions of these groups changed, but their Real American identity—their belief in themselves as the bedrock of self-government, not just one class among many as in a European society—stayed firm. From time to time the common people's politics has been interracial—the Populist Party at its founding in the early 1890s, the industrial labor movement of the 1930s—but it never lasted. The unity soon disintegrated under the pressure of white supremacy. Real America has always needed to feel that both a shiftless underclass and a parasitic elite depend on its labor. In this way it renders the Black working class invisible.

From its beginnings Real America has also been religious, and in a particular way—evangelical and fundamentalist, hostile to modern ideas and intellectual authority. The truth will enter every simple heart, and it doesn't come in shades of gray. "If we have to give up either religion or education, we should give up education," said Bryan, in whom populist democracy and fundamentalist Christianity were joined until they broke him apart at the Scopes Monkey Trial in 1925.

Finally, Real America has a strong nationalist character.

Its attitude toward the rest of the world is isolationist, hostile to humanitarianism and international engagement, but ready to respond aggressively to any incursion against national interests. The purity and strength of Americanism are always threatened by contamination from outside and betrayal from within. The narrative of Real America is white Christian nationalism.

Real America isn't a shining city on a hill with its gates open to freedom-loving people everywhere. Nor is it a cosmopolitan club where the right talents and credentials will get you admitted no matter who you are or where you're from. It's a provincial village where everyone knows everyone's business, no one has much more money than anyone else, and only a few misfits ever move away. The villagers can fix their own boilers, and they go out of their way to help a neighbor in a jam. A new face on the street will draw immediate attention and suspicion.

By the time Palin talked about "the real America," it was in precipitous decline. The region where she spoke, the North Carolina Piedmont, had lost its three economic mainstays—tobacco, textiles, and furniture making—in a single decade. Local people blamed NAFTA, multinational corporations, and big government. Idle tobacco farmers who had owned and worked their own fields drank vodka out of plastic cups at the Moose Lodge, where Fox News aired nonstop; they were missing teeth from using crystal meth. Palin's glowing remarks were a generation out of date. A great inversion had occurred. The dangerous, depraved cities gradually became safe for clean-living professional families, while heartland towns succumbed to pathologies usually associated with the Black inner cities: intergenerational poverty, disability, bankruptcy, out-of-wedlock births, addiction, prison, social distrust, political cynicism, unhappiness, early death.

This collapse happened in the shadow of historic failures. In the first decade of the new century, the bipartisan ruling class discredited itself—first overseas, then at home. The invasion of Iraq squandered the national unity and international sympathy that followed the attacks of September 11. The decision itself was a strategic folly enabled by lies and self-deception; the botched execution compounded the disaster for years afterward. The price was never paid by the war's leaders. As a U.S. Army officer in Iraq wrote in 2007, "A private who loses a rifle suffers far greater consequences than a general who loses a war." The cost for Americans fell on the bodies and minds of young men and women from small towns and inner cities. It was unusual to meet anyone in uniform in Iraq who came from a family of educated professionals, and vanishingly rare in the enlisted ranks. The memorials in Ivy League universities, with their long honor rolls from every war up until Vietnam, have few names to add from the post-9/11 conflicts. The credentialed Americans in Iraq were more likely diplomats, aid specialists, consultants, and journalists. Almost all of them returned home intact to move on to other pursuits. I was one.

After Iraq subsided, the pattern continued in Afghanistan.

The inequality of sacrifice in the global war on terror was almost too normal to bear comment. But this grand elite failure seeded cynicism in the young downscale generation.

The financial crisis of 2008, and the Great Recession that followed, had a similar effect on the home front. The guilty parties were elites—bankers, traders, regulators, and policy-makers. Alan Greenspan, the Federal Reserve chairman and an Ayn Rand fan, admitted that the crisis undermined his faith in the narrative of Free America. But those who did the suffering were lower down the class structure: middle-class Americans whose wealth was sunk in a house that lost half its value and a retirement fund that melted away; working-class Americans thrown into poverty by a pink slip. The banks received bailouts and the bankers kept their jobs. The economic collapse was triggered by fraud, but no financier was ever charged with a crime. A Wall Street trader told me that the crisis had been "a speed bump" in his world.

The conclusion was obvious: The system was rigged for insiders. The economic recovery took years; the recovery of trust never came.

These failures produced two political uprisings, two re-bellions against the party establishments. One, on the left, was Occupy Wall Street. It flared up and just as quickly flamed out, with an afterglow. On the right, the Tea Party lasted longer and forced concrete political changes, always negative ones. Its harsh attitude toward government pro-grams was close enough to the narrative of Free America that the Republican establishment was able, with difficulty, to absorb the Tea Party. But its nihilistic spirit accelerated the party's decline.

Ever since Reagan, the Republican Party has been a coalition of business interests and downscale whites, many of them evangelical Christians. By 2010 it was like a figure in a hall of mirrors whose head and body have been severed but continue to move as if they're still attached. The persistence of the coalition required an immense amount of self-deception on both sides. Mitt Romney, a rich investor who benefited from cheap immigrant labor, had to pretend to be outraged by undocumented workers. Midwestern retirees who depended on social security had to ignore the fact that the representatives they kept electing, such as the libertarian Paul Ryan, wanted to slash their benefits. Veterans of Iraq and Afghanistan returned to Indiana and Texas embittered at having lost their youth in unwinnable wars, while conservative pundits kept demanding new ones. A Tea Party protester at a town hall meeting on Obamacare shouted, "Keep your government hands off my Medicare!" These contradictions were headed for a reckoning.

As late as 2012, the Republican convention (in Tampa) was still a celebration of Free America and unfettered capitalism. Romney told donors at a fundraiser that the country was divided into makers and takers, and the 47 percent of Americans who took would never vote for him. His audience must have imagined the usual suspects in the Democratic cities. In fact, there were plenty of Republicans among the takers. Out in the decaying countryside, white Americans also resented the "freeloaders" among their own struggling kin and neighbors. The anti-government rhetoric of Free America still held, but the disorganization of life in Real America betrayed its emptiness. Politicians and journalists barely noticed the change. Christians who didn't attend church; workers without a regular schedule, let alone a union; renters who didn't trust their neighbors; children going to school online; adults who got their information from email chains and fringe websites; voters who believed both parties to be corrupt—what was the news story? Real America, the bedrock of popular democracy, had no way to participate in self-government. It turned out to be disposable. Its rage and despair needed a voice.

When Trump ran for president, the party of Free America collapsed into its own hollowness. The mass of Republicans were not constitutional originalists, libertarian free traders, members of the Federalist Society, or devout readers of *The Wall Street Journal*. They wanted government to do things that benefited *them*—not the undeserving classes below and above them. Party elites were too remote from Trump's supporters and lulled by their own stale rhetoric to grasp what was happening. Media elites were just as stupefied. They were entertained and appalled by Trump, and they dismissed him as a racist, a sexist, a xenophobe, an authoritarian, and a vulgar orange-haired celebrity. He was all of these. But he had a reptilian genius for intuiting the emotions of Real America—terra incognita to elites on the right and left. They were helpless to understand Trump and therefore to stop him.

Trump violated conservative orthodoxy on numerous issues, including taxes and entitlements. "I want to save the middle class," he said. "The hedge-fund guys didn't build this country. These are guys that shift paper around and they get lucky." But Trump's main heresies were on trade, immigration, and war. He was the first American politician to succeed by running against globalization—a bipartisan policy that had served the interests of "globalists" for years while sacrificing Real Americans. He was also the first to succeed by talking about how shitty everything in America had become. "These are the forgotten men and women of our country, and they *are* forgotten," he said at the Republican convention in Cleveland. "But they're not going to be forgotten long." The nationalist mantle was lying around, and Trump grabbed it. "*I am your voice.*"

Early in the campaign, I spent time with a group of white and Black steelworkers in a town near Canton, Ohio. They had been locked out by the company over a contract dispute and were picketing outside the mill. They faced months without a paycheck, possibly the loss of their jobs, and they talked about the end of the middle class. The only candidates who interested them were Trump and Bernie Sanders (one of the workers was reading Thomas Piketty's *Capital in the Twenty-First Century*). No one even mentioned the two establishment favorites, Hillary Clinton and Jeb Bush.

A steelworker named Jack Baum told me that he was supporting Trump. He liked Trump's "patriotic" positions on trade and immigration, but he also found Trump's insults refreshing, even exhilarating. The ugliness was a kind of re-venge, Baum said: "It's a mirror of the way *they* see *us*." He didn't specify who *they* and *us* were, but maybe he didn't have to. Maybe he believed—he was far too respectful to say it—that people like me looked down on people like him. If educated professionals considered steelworkers like Jack Baum to be ignorant, crass, and bigoted, then Trump was going to shove it in our smug faces. The lower his language and behavior sank, and the more the media vilified him, the more he was celebrated by his people. He was their leader, who could do no wrong.

What was Trump? A fascist? A white nationalist? A malig-nant narcissist? A conservative with very bad manners? Once he became president, his only legislative achievement—a huge tax cut that heavily favored the rich and corporations—fit right in with Republican orthodoxy. His court appoint-ments were friendly to business interests and also to religious traditionalists, while his actions on trade, immigration, and foreign conflicts had limited effects. By this view, Trump was a tool of big capitalists. The power-hungry leaders of Free America used Trump's presidency and his political failings to squeeze more plunder out of the economy and more breath out of government by the people. This describes what hap-pened under Trump, but it doesn't account for what made him new and powerful. He represented a social and political phenomenon that eludes standard left/right categories.

Was he then a fascist with a Queens accent? Some of Trump's advisors, like Steve Bannon, claimed inspiration from European reactionaries of the twenties and thirties. At times the cocked-chin Trump seemed to style himself after Mussolini or Franco. In 2017 he gave a speech before a rapturous crowd in Warsaw on the enemies of Western civilization, and you can almost picture him in a white uniform with gold braid and a red sash: "Americans, Poles, and the nations of Europe value individual freedom and sovereignty. We must work together to confront forces, whether they come from inside or out, from the South or the East, that threaten over time to undermine these values and to erase the bonds of culture, faith, and tradition that make us who we are."

"Culture, faith, and tradition." Trump never talked about self-government. He was the first American president who routinely trashed democracy.

But "fascist" puts him in an ideological mold that he doesn't deserve. If Trump were a fascist, he would have used the pandemic to seize control of industry, suspend individual liberties, and place the public under a regime of strict surveillance. In fascism, capitalism serves the state, not the other way around. The fascists were a vanguard of the future. They whipped up collective energies for visionary national goals—full employment, rearmament, conquest, and genocide. Look at pictures of fascist rallies. The faces in the crowd are ecstatic, the masses feel themselves elevated, they're ready to undertake superhuman feats of exertion for the leader, risk their lives, give their lives. Americans came to Trump's rallies for the fun, the red meat. The expression on their faces was a gleeful snarl. Nothing whatsoever was asked of them—not even to stick around until Trump had finished. His speeches didn't have a breath of inspiration.

Trump's language was effective because it was attuned to American pop culture. It required no expert knowledge and had no code of hidden meanings. It gave rise almost spontaneously to memorable phrases—"Make America great again," "Drain the swamp," "Build the wall," "Lock her up," "Send her back." It's the way people talk when the inhibitors are off, and available to anyone willing to join the mob. He didn't try to shape his people ideologically with new words and concepts. He used the low language of talk radio, reality TV, social media, and sports bars, and to his listeners this language seemed far more honest and grounded in common sense than the mincing obscurities of "politically correct" experts. His populism brought the cynical cruelty of *Jersey Shore* to national politics. The goal of his speeches was not to whip up mass hysteria but to get rid of shame. He leveled everyone down together.

The deeper problem with Trump as a fascist is that it lets the rest of society off the hook. It gives his opponents a heroic role to play. If Trump was Mussolini, we were the "resistance." Trump's presidency was imposed on us like a dictatorship, and we congratulated ourselves for spending four years addicted to the pleasure of obsessively denouncing him. We don't have to ask ourselves how we let him happen.

"White nationalist" comes closer. Throughout his adult

life Trump was hostile to Black people, contemptuous of women, vicious about immigrants from poor countries, and cruel toward the weak. He was an equal-opportunity bigot. In his campaigns and in the White House he aligned himself publicly with hard-core racists in a way that set him apart from every president in memory, and the racists loved him for it. Trump's noxious statements raised the question of whether those who voted for him in 2016—63 million Americans—were also bigots. After the election a great deal of journalism and social science was devoted to finding out whether Trump's voters were mainly motivated by economic anxiety or racial resentment. There was evidence for both answers.

Progressives, shocked by the readiness of half the country to support this hateful man, seized on racism as the single cause and set out to disprove every alternative. But this answer was far too satisfying. Racism is such an irreducible evil that it gave progressives the commanding moral heights and relieved them of the burden of understanding the motives of their compatriots down in the lowlands, let alone doing something about them. It put Trump's voters beyond the pale. But how did racism explain why white men were much more likely to vote for Trump than white women, and why the same was true of Black men and women? Or why the most reliable factor for Trump voters wasn't race but the combination of race and education? Among whites, 38 percent of college graduates voted for Trump, compared with 64 percent without college degrees. This margin—the vast gap between Smart America and Real America—was the decisive one. It made 2016 different from previous elections, and the trend only intensified in 2020.

Trump's voters were not the wretched of the earth. They were generally ill-educated, living far from prosperous cities in nearly all-white communities, employed in sectors on the downward slope of the economy, gloomy about their own and their children's prospects, ready to think nonwhites were cutting in line or taking a free ride, threatened by competition from immigrants, and enraged by contemptuous elites who made rules that benefited only themselves. It isn't necessary to choose among race, class, culture, and social status to understand why Trump won. It was all of them together, reinforcing one another.

The most persuasive description of Trump's ordinary supporters appeared just after the 2020 election, in a reader's comment on a *New York Times* op-ed that had attributed his 74 million votes to white supremacy:

> I grew up in rural America. My home county went 80–20 for Trump. I also spent 6 months in my hometown since the 2016 election.
>
> I'm here to tell you: under-education + lack of faith in the political and economic system that has failed them + Christianity + 40 years of conservatism becoming more and more extreme + right wing talk radio + virtually no mental healthcare + lack of interaction with anyone outside of their race mixed with stereotypes that have become

"normalized" + social media + no good jobs + poor health from over-work/dangerous jobs + economic desperation x **magical savior** = trumpism.

I voted for Biden. I hope he can help my hometown, and the distressed people in it. Trumpism is a cult now. There is work to be done to fix this.

Here's what you can do: you can overcome your classist views . . . A field trip outside of your city might help. Maybe try volunteering in Trump country: help! teach! feed! befriend! These are your fellow Americans and they are hurting.

What started with Palin was consummated with Trump. American politics has always been dominated by white people, but for Trump's core supporters race became a matter of self-conscious identity. More Americans voted for Trump than just white people, and not all white people wanted membership, but white identity politics became the base of Trump's support. As with all identity politics, it drew on a sense of grievance and inequality. It was moved not by universal principles or concrete policies, but by the group's fear of the other and desire for power over its enemies. Those enemies were not just nonwhites, but anti-Trump Americans in general. Eventually white identity politics became Trump identity politics.

The issues Trump had campaigned on waxed and waned during his presidency. What remained was the dark energy he unleashed, binding him like a tribal leader to his people. Nothing was left of the optimistic pieties of Free America. Trump's people still talked about freedom, but they meant blood and soil. Their nationalism was like the ethno-nationalisms on the rise in Europe and around the world. Trump abused every American institution—the FBI, the CIA, the armed forces, the courts, the press, the Constitution itself—and his people cheered. Nothing, least of all making America great again, excited them like owning the libs. Nothing persuaded them like Trump's 30,000 lies.

How did practical, hands-on, self-reliant Americans, still balancing family budgets and following complex repair manuals, slip into such cognitive decline when it came to politics? Blaming ignorance or stupidity would be a mistake. You have to summon an act of will, a desperate energy and imagination, to replace truth with the authority of a con man like Trump. The mob that stormed the Capitol was the lonely modern masses described by Hannah Arendt in *The Origins of Totalitarianism*. They are cut off from their fellow citizens and from reality itself, some sworn to a hateful ideology, some longing for an identity that can deliver them from the unbearable condition of "their essential homelessness." They found an identity in their leader. They surrendered the ability to think for themselves, and with it the capacity for self-government. They became litter swirling in the wind of any preposterous claim that blew from @realdonaldtrump. Truth was whatever made the world whole again by hurting their enemies— the more far-fetched, the truer.

More than anything, Trump was a demagogue—a

thoroughly American type, familiar to us from novels like *All the King's Men* and movies like *Citizen Kane*. "Trump is a creature native to our own style of government and therefore much more difficult to protect ourselves against," the Yale political theorist Bryan Garsten wrote. "He is a demagogue, a popular leader who feeds on the hatred of elites that grows naturally in democratic soil." A demagogue can become a tyrant, but it's the people who put him there—the people who want to be fed fantasies and lies, the people who set themselves apart from and above their compatriots. So the question is not who Trump was, but who we are.

4.

In 2014 American character changed.

A large and influential generation came of age in the shadow of accumulating failures by the ruling class—especially by business and foreign policy elites. This new generation had little faith in ideas that previous ones were raised on: All men are created equal. Work hard and you can be anything. Knowledge is power. Democracy and capitalism are the best systems—the *only* systems. America is a nation of immigrants. America is the leader of the free world.

My generation told our children's generation a story of slow but steady progress. America had slavery (as well as genocide, internment, and other crimes) to answer for, original sin if there ever was such a thing—but it *had* answered, and with the civil rights movement the biggest barriers to equality were overcome. If anyone doubted that the country was becoming a more perfect union, the election of a Black president who loved to use that phrase proved it. "Rosa sat so Martin could walk so Obama could run so we could all fly": that was the story in a sentence, and it was so convincing to a lot of people in my generation—including me—that we were slow to notice how little it meant to a lot of people under thirty-five. Or we heard but didn't understand and dismissed them with irritable mental gestures. We told them they had no idea what the crime rate was like in 1994. Smart Americans pointed to affirmative action and children's health insurance. Free Americans touted enterprise zones and school vouchers.

Of course the kids didn't buy it. In their eyes "progress" looked like a thin upper layer of Black celebrities and professionals, who carried the weight of society's expectations along with its prejudices, and below them, lousy schools, overflowing prisons, dying neighborhoods. The parents didn't really buy it either, but we had learned to ignore injustice on this scale as adults ignore so much just to get through. If anyone could smell out the bad faith of parents, it was their children, underage, stressed-out laborers in the multigenerational family business of success, bearing the psychological burdens of the meritocracy. Many of them, loaded with debt, entered the workforce just as the Great Recession closed off opportunities and the reality of planetary destruction bore down on them. No wonder their digital lives seemed more real to them than the world of their parents. No wonder they had less sex than previous generations. No wonder the bland promises of middle-aged liberals left them furious.

Then came one video after another of police killing or hurting unarmed Black people. Then came the election of an openly racist president. These were conditions for a generational revolt.

Call its narrative *Just America*. It's another rebellion from below. As Real America breaks down the ossified libertarianism of Free America, Just America assaults the complacent meritocracy of Smart America. It does the hard, essential thing that the other three narratives avoid, that white Americans have avoided throughout our history. It forces us to see the straight line that runs from slavery and segregation to the second-class life so many Black Americans live today—the betrayal of equality that has always been the country's great moral shame, the dark heart of its social problems.

But Just America has a dissonant sound, for in its narrative justice and America never rhyme. A more accurate name would be Unjust America, in a spirit of attack rather than aspiration. For Just Americans, the country is less a project of self-government to be improved than a site of continuous wrong to be battled. In some versions of the narrative, the country has no positive value at all—it can never be made better.

In the same way that libertarian ideas had been lying around for Americans to pick up in the stagflated 1970s, young people coming of age in the disillusioned 2000s were handed powerful ideas about social justice to explain their world. These ideas came from different intellectual traditions: the Frankfurt School for Social Research in 1920s Germany, French postmodernist thinkers of the 1960s and '70s, radical feminism, and Black studies. They converged and recombined in American university classrooms, where two generations of students were taught to think as critical theorists.

Critical theory upends the universal values of the Enlightenment: objectivity, rationality, science, equality and freedom of the individual. These liberal values are an ideology by which dominant groups subjugate other groups. All relations are power relations, everything is political, and claims of reason and truth are social constructs that maintain those in power. Unlike orthodox Marxism, critical theory is concerned with language and identity more than with material conditions. In place of objective reality, critical theorists place subjectivity at the center of analysis to show how supposedly universal terms exclude oppressed groups and help the powerful rule over them. Critical theorists argue that the Enlightenment, including the American founding, carried the seeds of modern racism and imperialism.

The term "identity politics" was born in 1977, when a group of Black lesbian feminists called the Combahee River Collective released a statement defining their work as self-liberation from "white male rule" under both racism and sexism: "The major systems of oppression are interlocking.

The synthesis of these oppressions creates the conditions of our lives . . . This focusing upon our own oppression is embodied in the concept of identity politics. We believe that the most profound and potentially most radical politics come directly out of our own identity." The statement helped to set in motion a way of thinking that places the struggle for justice within the self. This thinking appeals to authority, not reason or universal values—the authority of identity, the "lived experience" of the oppressed. The self is not a rational being that can persuade and be persuaded by other selves, because reason is another form of power. Each self is a point where different identities intersect, and the oppressed live at the confluence of different systems of oppression (it was another decade before the term "intersectionality" was coined). Over time the categories of identity grew—from race and sex to sexuality, gender, religion, disability, body type. In each category the oppressed group has its counterpart in an oppressor.

The historical demand of the oppressed is inclusion as equal citizens in all the institutions of American life. With identity politics, the demand became different: not just to enlarge the institutions, but to change them profoundly. When Martin Luther King, Jr., at the March on Washington, called on America to "rise up and live out the true meaning of its creed: 'We hold these truths to be self-evident, that all men are created equal,'" he was demanding equal rights within the framework of the Enlightenment (toward the end of his life, his view of the American creed grew more complicated).

But in identity politics, equality refers to groups, not individuals. All disparities between groups result from systems of oppression and demand collective action for redress, often amounting to new forms of discrimination—in other words, equity. In practice, identity politics inverts the old hierarchy of power into a new one: bottom rail on top. The fixed lens of power makes true equality, based on common humanity, impossible.

And what is oppression? Not unjust laws—the most important ones were overturned by the civil rights movement and its successors—or even unjust living conditions. The focus on subjectivity moves oppression from the world to the self and its pain—psychological trauma, harm from speech and texts, the sense of alienation that minorities feel in constant exposure to a dominant culture. A whole system of oppression can exist within a single word.

By the turn of the millennium these ideas were nearly ubiquitous in humanities and social science departments. Embracing them had become an important credential for admittance into sectors of the professorate. The ideas gave scholars an irresistible power, intellectual and moral, to criticize institutions in which they were comfortably embedded. In turn, these scholars formed the worldview of young Americans educated by elite universities to thrive in the meritocracy, students trained from early childhood to do what it takes to succeed professionally and socially. The students looked up to experts, and so they looked up to their professors. Perhaps because twenty-year-olds are preoccupied with finding their own identity in the world, they made a receptive audience.

"It is a curious thing," D. H. Lawrence wrote, "but the ideas of one generation become the instincts of the next." The ideas of critical theorists became the instincts of millennials. It wasn't necessary to have read Foucault or studied under Judith Butler to become adept with terms like "centered," "marginalized," "privilege," and "harm"; to believe that words can be a form of violence; to close down a general argument with a personal truth ("you wouldn't understand," or just "I'm offended"); to keep your mouth shut when identity disqualified you from speaking. Millions of young Americans were steeped in the assumptions of critical theory and identity politics without knowing the concepts. Everyone sensed their power. Not everyone resisted the temptation to abuse it.

For years the concepts stayed on campus. Now and then a news story reached the outside world with accounts of an academic culture practicing strange rites of accusation and inquisition. Students demanded "trigger warnings" to steer them clear of upsetting passages in books like *The Great Gatsby* and *Mrs. Dalloway*. They protested "cultural appropriation" in the Vietnamese sandwiches prepared by dining hall workers (banh mi is made with grilled pork and pickled vegetables on a baguette, *not* pulled pork and coleslaw on ciabatta). The $12-an-hour dining hall workers reacted with bemusement, or sullen rage.

These incidents of "political correctness," amplified by right-wing media, whipped up hatred of elites out in Real

America. The culture wars raged on, as bloody-minded and durable as the Thirty Years' War, a full-employment program for pundits of every type. Some worried about a generation of ultra-sensitive children coddled by ultra-indulgent adults. Others dismissed the worry as a lot of hand-wringing over kids being kids. Wise heads in Smart America said, "Wait till they find out how the world really works." But it was the world that changed, not the students.

The change began in 2014. That was the year when the views of some Americans—white Democrats and people with college degrees—took a sharp turn to the left on identity issues. *Is bias the main cause of racial inequality? Do slavery and past discrimination still hold Black people back today? Do immigrants strengthen the country because of their hard work and talents?* The percentage of white college graduates answering yes to questions like these suddenly shot upward. It's worth noting that the views of Black Democrats didn't change nearly as much. It's also worth noting that Republicans were becoming slightly more progressive on these issues, until the election of Donald Trump two years later. Then a polarizing dialectic set in, as his supporters and opponents drove each other to extremes, identity politics against identity politics, replicating endlessly.

It's hard to say why Just America emerged as a national narrative in 2014. That summer, in Ferguson, Missouri, a white police officer shot and killed an eighteen-year-old

Black man, whose body was left to lie on the street for hours. Though the details were ambiguous—the victim, Michael Brown, had attacked the cop, Darren Wilson—the symbolism overwhelmed evenhanded analysis. The killing came in the context of numerous incidents, increasingly caught on video, of Black people assaulted and killed by white police who had faced no obvious threat. And those videos, widely distributed on social media and viewed millions of times, symbolized the wider injustices that still confronted Black Americans in prisons and neighborhoods and schools and workplaces—in the sixth year of the first Black presidency. The optimistic story of incremental progress and expanding opportunity in a multiracial society collapsed, seemingly overnight. The incident in Ferguson ignited a protest movement in cities and campuses around the country.

It came under the rubric of social justice. It was a young movement, overwhelmingly people under forty, and especially the well educated. In identity they found a sense of meaning and community, a way out of the anomie of digital consumerism, that nothing else in liberal capitalist America gave them.

What is the narrative of Just America? It sees American society not as mixed and fluid, ever more so through time, but as a fixed hierarchy, like a caste system. (*Caste* is the title of one of the most popular books of Just America; two others are *The New Jim Crow* and *Stamped from the Beginning*.) In the words of William Faulkner, for Just America, "The past is never dead. It's not even past." An outpouring of prize-winning books, essays, journalism, films, poetry, pop music, and scholarly work looks to the history of slavery and segregation in order to understand the present—as if to say, "Not so fast." The most famous of this work, *The New York Times Magazine*'s 1619 Project, declared its ambition to retell the entire story of America as the story of slavery and its consequences, tracing every contemporary phenomenon to its historical antecedent in racism, sometimes in disregard of contradictory facts. Any talk of progress is false consciousness—even "hurtful." Whatever the actions of this or that individual, whatever new laws and practices come along, the hierarchical position of "whiteness" over "Blackness" is eternal.

Here is the revolutionary power of the narrative: What had been considered, broadly speaking, American history (or literature, philosophy, classics, even math) is explicitly defined as white, and therefore supremacist. What was innocent by default suddenly finds itself on trial, every idea is cross-examined, and nothing else can get done until the case is heard.

Just America isn't only concerned with race. Some followers of the narrative are socialists and environmentalists, and they devote their efforts to minimum-wage laws and green energy. Some care passionately about sexism. Some are militants for abolishing the biological definition of gender. The most radical version of the narrative lashes together the oppression of all groups in an encompassing hell of white supremacy, patriarchy, homophobia and transphobia, plutocracy, environmental destruction, and drones—America as a unitary malignant force beyond any other evil on earth. The end of Ta-Nehisi Coates's *Between the World and Me*, published in 2015 and hugely influential in establishing the narrative of Just America, interprets global warming as the planet's cosmic revenge on white people for their greed and cruelty.

But fundamentally Just America *is* about race. Everything else is adjunct. Occupy Wall Street lasted a few months, but Black Lives Matter keeps gathering strength year by year. In 2020, when the New York chapter of the Democratic Socialists of America learned that its invited speaker, the eminent Black political scientist Adolph Reed, intended to discuss class politics in opposition to racial politics, his appearance was canceled. Even some socialists refuse to discuss class without talking about race.

But talking about race rarely gets to the heart of the matter. The talk is crippled by fear, shame, hurt, anger, politeness, posturing, self-censorship, self-flagellation, and the inability of flawed human beings to rise to the subject's huge demands. No one says what they think when the setting is a university classroom, an anti-bias training session, a newspaper op-ed, or a tweet. These are all performance spaces. It would be better to have *real* conversations, two people of different races alone in a room together, speaking, listening, responding, on and on, for an hour or two or three, *telling the truth*. Do it with a hundred different pairs, film the conversations, disguise the identities of the participants, and stream them unedited on YouTube. The project would achieve more than all the bestsellers and workshops in the world.

There are too many things that Just America can't talk about for the narrative to get at the hardest problems. It can't talk about the complex causes of poverty. Structural racism—ongoing disadvantages that Black people suffer from policies and institutions over the centuries—is real. So is individual agency, but in the Just America narrative it doesn't exist. The narrative can't talk about the main source of violence in Black neighborhoods, which is young Black men, not police. The push to "defund the police" in Minneapolis and other cities during the George Floyd protests was stopped by local Black citizens, who wanted better, not less, policing. Just America can't deal with the stubborn divide between Black and white students in academic assessments. The mild phrase "achievement gap" has been banished, not just because it implies that Black parents and children have some responsibility but also because, according to anti-racist ideology, any disparity is by definition racist, as is any attempt to analyze the disparity with other terms. Get rid of assessments and you'll end the racism along with the gap.

I'm exaggerating the suddenness of this new narrative, but not by much. It's astonishing how quickly things changed after 2014, when Just America escaped campus and pervaded the wider culture. First, the "softer" professions gave way. Book publishers released a torrent of titles on race and identity, and year after year those books won the most prestigious prizes. Newspapers and magazines known for aspiring to reportorial objectivity shifted toward an activist model of journalism, adopting new values and assumptions along with a brand-new language: *systemic racism, white supremacy, white privilege, anti-Blackness, marginalized communities, decolonize, toxic masculinity, nonbinary, transphobia.* Similar changes came to arts organizations, philanthropies, scientific institutions, technology monopolies, and finally corporate America and the Democratic Party. The incontestable principle of inclusion drove the changes, making them a powerful force toward a more perfect union, but they smuggled in more threatening features that have come to characterize identity politics and social justice: monolithic group thought, hostility to open debate, and a taste for moral coercion.

Just America has dramatically changed the way Americans think, talk, and act, but not the conditions in which they live. It reflects the fracturing distrust that defines our culture: *Something is deeply wrong; our society is unjust; our institutions are corrupt.* If the narrative helps to create a more humane criminal justice system and bring Black Americans into the conditions of full equality, it will live up to its promise. But the grand systemic analysis usually ends in small symbolic politics. In some ways Just America resembles Real America and has entered the same dubious conflict from the other side. The disillusionment with liberal capitalism that gave rise to identity politics has also produced a new authoritarianism among many young white men. Just and Real America share a skepticism, from opposing points of view, about the universal ideas of the founding documents and the promise of America as a multi-everything democracy.

There's another way to understand Just America, like the other three narratives, and that's in terms of class. Why does so much of its work take place in human resources departments, reading lists, and awards ceremonies? In the summer of 2020 the protesters in the streets of New York were disproportionately white millennials with advanced degrees making more than $100,000 a year. Just America is a narrative of the young and well-educated, which is why it continually misreads or ignores the Black and Latino working classes. The fate of this generation of young professionals has been cursed by economic stagnation and technological upheaval. The jobs their parents took for granted have become much harder to get, which makes the meritocratic rat race even more crushing. Law, medicine, academia, media— the most desirable professions—have all contracted, and in some cases, such as journalism, it's almost impossible to get in the door without the highest credentials and best connections. The result is a large population of overeducated, underemployed young people living in metropolitan areas.

The historian Peter Turchin coined the phrase "elite overproduction" to describe this phenomenon. He found that a constant source of instability and violence in previous eras of history, such as the late Roman Empire and the French Wars of Religion, was the frustration of social elites for whom there were not enough jobs. Turchin expects this country to undergo a similar breakdown in the coming decade. Just

America attracts surplus elites and channels most of their anger at the narrative to which they're closest—Smart America. The social justice movement is a repudiation of meritocracy, a rebellion against the system handed down from parents to children. Students at elite universities no longer believe they deserve their coveted slots. Activists in New York want to abolish the tests that determine entry into the city's most competitive high schools (where Asian American children now predominate). In some niche areas, such as literary magazines and graduate schools of education, any idea of merit separate from identity no longer exists.

But confessing racial privilege is a way to hang on to class privilege. Most Just Americans still belong to the meritocracy and have no desire to give up its advantages. They can't escape the status anxieties of Smart America—only they've transferred them to the new narrative. They want to be the first to adopt its expert terminology. In the summer of 2020 people suddenly began saying "BIPOC" as if they'd been doing it all their lives. ("Black Indigenous People of Color" was a way to uncouple groups that had been aggregated under "people of color" and give them their rightful place in the moral order, with everyone from Bogotá to Karachi to Seoul bringing up the rear.) The whole atmosphere of Just America at its most constricted—the fear of failing to say the right thing, the urge to level withering fire on minor faults—is a variation on the fierce competitive spirit of Smart America. It's the terms of accreditation that have changed. And, because achievement is a fragile basis for moral identity, when meritocrats are accused of racism they have no solid faith in their own worth to stand on.

In the summer of 2020, the protests against police brutality opened up a second front, in America's cultural institutions. Right when a mass movement for far-reaching reforms on behalf of an oppressed lower class seemed possible, Just America went for a revolution in consciousness and turned to the problem of diversity in elite organizations. Feelings ran high. There were uprisings from within, from the young—a frightening prospect to aging meritocrats trying to keep their jobs and their heads. They did what elites have always done when they come under attack from below and lose confidence in their right to lead. Smart America abdicated to Just America.

It happened in different ways across dozens of institutions almost simultaneously. Here are two examples, days apart in June.

At the beginning of the month, the *Times* published an op-ed by Senator Tom Cotton of Arkansas, arguing for the use of the U.S. military to put down rioting and looting—a view supported by about half the American people, including a large minority of Black Americans. *Times* employees were appalled, and they posted hundreds of tweets that all said the same thing: "Running this puts Black @nytimes staff in danger." This language, advised by their union, allowed them to go public with an editorial grievance without violating *Times* policy, since the complaint was framed in terms of workplace safety. But the statement was at least a wild surmise, if not simply false. The *Times* higher-ups tried to calm the storm with standard talk of airing counterarguments and improving the editorial process, but they were just buying time. Nothing would restore the standing of the publisher, A. G. Sulzberger—heir to the family business, the ultimate example of white male privilege—short of buying an indulgence by firing the senior editor responsible for the op-ed, whatever the merits of its publication.

This professional execution sent an unmistakable message, not just to the paper but to the world of journalism: the rules in Just America are different. The parameters of publishable opinion are a lot narrower than they used to be. A written thought can be a form of violence. The loudest public voices in a controversy will prevail. Offending them can cost your career. Justice is power. These new rules are not based on liberal values; they are post-liberal.

The same revolution was happening in the arts. Later in June, *Poetry*, the country's most prominent and wealthy journal of poetry, published "Scholls Ferry Rd." by Michael Dickman. The poem conveyed the mental decline of the poet's grandmother in fragments of imagery and dialogue, including these lines:

"Negress" was another word she liked to use

That's the nice way to say it

"Oh they are always changing what they want to be called"

On the bus she dropped her purse

I was with her
A nice Negress handed it back

She put out her hand to receive it the whole time looking out
the window
                                        never said a word

It was a poem in the modern tradition—indirection, irony, shifting voice—that has defined *Poetry* from its founding in 1912 and its publication of T. S. Eliot's "Love Song of J. Alfred Prufrock" in 1915. But a twenty-year-old premed student and aspiring poet read these lines and confronted the magazine on Twitter: "It's pretty unacceptable that you would publish this, especially during a time when so many POC are grieving/being targeted. Shouldn't you be focusing on amplifying Black voices right now?" Hundreds of outraged readers chimed in. They were not famous, but their collective scorn gave them power.

Within a day *Poetry*'s editor, Don Share, resigned. Not long before, in an interview, he had expressed an anti-doctrinaire approach to poetry: "In the long term, the best poems, and the best poets, if we use such terms, are unaccountable and ultimately unignorable." But in a letter of apology announcing his resignation, he confessed his doctrinal error. Poems are accountable to the narrative of Just America: "I had read the poem as one of condemnation. But this wishful thinking does not justify the fact that 'Scholls Ferry Rd.' egregiously voices offensive language that is neither specifically identified nor explicitly condemned as racist. It also centers completely on white voices, leaving room for no other presences. Because we read poetry to deepen our understanding of human otherness, I failed in my responsibility to understand that the poem I thought I was reading was not the one that people would actually read."

The abject tone, the eager adoption of his critics' terms: signs of philosophical surrender. A whole aesthetic of literary freedom and moral complexity collapsed overnight under the weight of a thousand tweets, as if it had been hollowing out for years. Share was among the cultural meritocrats not adept enough to survive the summer's uprising. The next issue of *Poetry*, fully converted to the new aesthetic, presented the literature of the future in a poem by Noor Hindi called "Fuck Your Lecture on Craft, My People Are Dying":

> *Colonizers write about flowers.*
> *I tell you about children throwing rocks at Israeli tanks*
> *seconds before becoming daisies . . .*
> *I know I'm American because when I walk into a room*
>   *something dies.*

The culture of Just America rejects the idea of any sphere of life autonomous from politics, specifically identity politics. In the name of inclusion it overthrows the liberal values of the previous generation, whose elites—because they no longer believe in those values, or because words like "justice" and "racism" freeze their tongues, or because they want to hold on to their places, or because it's humiliating to be old and irrelevant—offer no resistance.

In 1955, three years after the publication of *Invisible Man*, the novelist Ralph Ellison was interviewed by *The Paris Review*. "One function of serious literature is to deal with the moral core of a given society," he said. "Well, in the United States the Negro and his status have always stood for that moral concern. He symbolizes among other things the human and social possibility of equality. This is the moral question raised in our two great nineteenth-century novels, *Moby-Dick* and *Huckleberry Finn* . . . Perhaps the discomfort about protest in books by Negro authors comes because since the nineteenth century American literature has avoided profound moral searching. It was too painful."

In Ellison's words are clues to a narrative that could produce great literature as well as social justice. The word that jumps out is "equality." I think it holds a key. But Just America goes in a different direction, down a dead-end street. Its origins in theory, its intolerant dogma, and its coercive tactics remind me of left-wing ideology in the 1930s. Liberalism as white supremacy recalls the Communist Party's attack on social democracy as "social fascism." Woke aesthetics is the new socialist realism.

The dead end of Just America is a tragedy. This country has had great movements for justice in the past and badly needs one now. But in order to work it has to throw its arms out wide. It has to tell a story in which most of us can see ourselves, and start on a path that most of us want to follow.

All four of the narratives I've described emerged from America's failure to enlarge the middle-class democracy of the postwar years as a multi-everything democracy in this century. They all respond to real problems. Each offers a value that the others need and lacks ones that the others have. Free America celebrates the energy of the unencumbered individual. Smart America respects intelligence and welcomes change. Real America commits itself to a place and has a sense of limits. Just America demands a confrontation with what the others want to avoid. They rise from a single society, and even in one as polarized as ours they continually shape, absorb, and morph into one another. But their tendency is also to divide us up, pitting tribe against tribe. These divisions impoverish each narrative into a cramped and ever more extreme version of itself.

At the heart of our divisions is almost half a century of rising inequality and declining social mobility. Americans tolerate more economic inequality than citizens of other modern democracies: if anyone can become anything, today's unequal results are fair and might well change tomorrow. That was never completely true, but now it's plainly false. We have a stratified society in which not just wealth is unequal but also status, like a hereditary aristocracy in which some people are considered superior to others. We don't look each other in the face as fellow citizens.

In such a world, belief in equality is broken, while the desire for it still exists, stifled and smoldering, and this deforms our identity as Americans. All four narratives are driven by a competition for status—the consequence of this broken promise—that generates fierce anxiety and resentment. They all anoint winners and losers. In Free America the winners are the makers, and the losers are the takers who want to drag the rest down in perpetual dependency on a smothering government. In Smart America the winners are the credentialed meritocrats, and the losers are the poorly educated who want to resist inevitable progress. In Real America the winners are the hardworking folk of the white Christian heartland, and the losers are treacherous elites and contaminating others who want to destroy the country. In Just America the winners are the marginalized groups, and the losers are the dominant groups that wanted to go on dominating.

I don't much want to live in the republic of any of them.

The idea of governing ourselves as equals has lost its hold on us. It's always an ideal, never reached, often violated. But without it America doesn't work.

EQUAL AMERICA

Each of the two countries that the election of 2020 exposed is split by two narratives—Smart and Just on one side, Free and Real on the other. The tensions within each country will persist even as the cold civil war between them rages on. But the election, forcing a binary choice, temporarily consolidated the narratives on either side of the divide. In one country, cities are magnets for talent and ambition, higher education is the key to success in the information economy, diversity is a sign of progress, and Joe Biden is the legitimate president. In the other, the home fires of American greatness burn in aging towns and rural areas, the good jobs are in manufacturing, farming, and fuel extraction, diversity is shredding the national fabric, and Donald Trump was robbed. One country believes we narrowly averted the overthrow of democracy, and the other believes we saw its brazen perversion in a massive fraud. Each views the other as an existential enemy with whom compromise would be betrayal.

After the election, several prominent Republicans floated the possibility of secession. One of them was the late talk radio demagogue Rush Limbaugh: "I see more and more people asking, 'What in the world do we have in common with the people who live in, say, New York?'" This type of question isn't new. After Trump's victory in 2016, some Democrats openly wished that the southern states, his solid red base, had been allowed to secede in 1861. This wish wasn't just based on Electoral College math—it reflected a deep sense of estrangement, as if an alien country, full of heavily armed bigots and religious zealots, is appended to the American underbelly.

Books and articles are now regularly published about how the United States might escape this standoff before real civil war breaks out. A conservative Christian writer argues that red and blue states are so different, not just politically but culturally, and filled with so much mutual loathing, that they should be given broad powers by Washington to govern themselves independently in order to head off violent secession movements. Let California be California and Tennessee be Tennessee before anyone gets assassinated. Some progressive writers want to push things in the opposite direction: revise political institutions, maybe even abolish the Constitution, so that one side can win and the other lose, allowing a national blue majority to rule over a red minority.

These scenarios pose a choice between separation and conquest. What's the alternative? A decadent politics that solves no problems but gives partisans a permanent arena for performances of righteous vitriol. Endless dysfunction, probably violence. The divide far exceeds any policy disputes over immigration or policing. Political differences are conflicts of core identity, and the mutual antagonism has the quality of hatred that precedes sectarian war. After the election, it was easy to draw comparisons with the year 1860.

In 1897—after another bitter election, during another period of existential crisis, the Gilded Age—the novelist William Dean Howells observed: "We trust the republic with itself; that is, we trust one another, and we trust one another the most implicitly when we affirm the most clamorously, one half of us, that the other half is plunging the whole of us in irreparable ruin. That is merely our way of calling all to the duty we owe to each. It is not a very dignified way, but the entire nation is in the joke, and it is not so mischievous as it might seem." Is that what's happening today? A lot of noise in the service of the republic? Meet me at the barricades, traitor, loser, cuck, and we'll figure out how to keep the American experiment alive!

Trust? It doesn't feel that way. I see an image of a Trump rally shot from behind a man wearing a baseball hat with the letter "Q," for QAnon, sewn on the back—a conspiracy theory that believes leading Democrats are involved in child sex trafficking and other atrocities, a theory to which Trump nodded and a new Republican congresswoman subscribed—and I think: It's hopeless.

But actual secession is impossible. Even Rush Limbaugh admitted this after his listeners took him seriously. Look at the map: the red area of the country stretches from Idaho in the Northwest to Florida in the Southeast, separating blue regions on the coasts, in the Southwest, and in the upper Midwest that don't make up a contiguous bloc. Even the deep red South now has a light blue spot in the shape of Georgia. Illinois and Indiana, blue and red neighbors, have far more in common than Vermont and Hawaii, both cobalt blue, or North Dakota and Alabama, both ruby red. The deepest divisions aren't found between regions or even between states, but within states. Silicon Valley is much closer to the Research Triangle of North Carolina on the other side of the country than it is to the California Central Valley, ninety minutes away. The fundamental unit of political division is the county. (And this description misses non-conforming populations, such as Cuban Americans in Dade County, Florida, Republican hedge-fund managers in Fairfield County, Connecticut, and Black industrial workers in Wayne County, Michigan.) For decades, as Americans have sorted themselves geographically in political communities of the like-minded, the number of "landslide counties"— where the presidential election was decided by more than 20 percent—has been increasing exponentially across the country. In 2020 the total passed half of all counties. Radical federalism in the states wouldn't solve the electoral map or the conflicts that come with it. A soft secession would have to take place county by county, where a large majority of Americans now live with compatriots who think like them. Try arranging them into two countries.

The other path is conquest. Each side of the divide harbors a fantasy of winning. It imagines that the other side will eventually go away, whether through demographic change, repeated election defeats, the magical powers of a demagogue, or collective social suicide. On the blue side, winning looks like Sherman's March to the Sea—total victory, leaving the smoking ruins of Republican garrisons across the land. On the red side, winning looks like tactical brilliance against a bigger, stronger enemy who eventually loses the will to fight and withdraws. These fantasies are nourished by the politically homogeneous lives most of us live. Because of them, one side or the other (and sometimes, as in 2020, both) is perpetually shocked by reality. Elections never deliver the promised realignment—therefore, they have to be wrong and illegitimately won, by fraudulent ballots, foreign subversion, corporate dollars, viral disinformation, or by a vast conspiracy of politicians, officials, voting machine makers, judges, and journalists across the land. Anything but the will of the people!

For the past twenty years, progressives have been waiting for a rising tide of younger, better-educated, more diverse voters to swamp white conservative America and lift them to victory. Every time there's a clear Democratic win—2008, 2018—they see the tide coming closer. Instead, the next election reveals that nothing much has changed, the sea level remains the same, the country is still divided almost 50/50. This political whiplash has been going on so long that the authors of *The Emerging Democratic Majority*, published in 2002, have had to clarify their thesis several times.

Everyone knows that our system benefits a minority party against the will of a (small) majority. To gain the White House, either house of Congress, or the legislatures of swing states, Democrats—victors of seven of the last eight presidential popular votes—must win elections by several percentage points. The highest purpose of the Republican Party today is to hold on to power by undemocratic means. Two of these—voter suppression and extreme gerrymandering—can be remedied and in some cases have been. If the filibuster is abused to block needed legislation, get rid of it and blame Aaron Burr that it ever existed. Circumvent the Electoral College through a compact among states—fifteen have already signed on—to cast their electors for the winner of the national popular vote. The Senate, an ancient corpse around the neck of democracy, is protected in perpetuity by Article 5 of the Constitution, which forbids any state from being deprived of "equal suffrage" without its consent. Still, statehood for D.C. would make the Senate more representative and enfranchise hundreds of thousands of Americans. Let the majority actually govern, let the people see the results, and the fever will subside. That's the conquest scenario. When I'm reading political news, I'm all for it.

But step back from Washington's daily atrocities and conquest seems less attractive or likely. It solves the political impasse but not the existential one. In the name of democracy it absolves itself of the democratic imperative to persuade. Putting a blue "coalition of transformation"—its most extreme and righteous impulses unchecked, and no need to listen—in power over a red "coalition of restoration" would leave the country unequal and ungovernable. The power would be legitimate, but it would not be very durable. "As I would not be a slave, so I would not be a master," Lincoln wrote in 1858. "This expresses my idea of democracy. Whatever differs from this, to the extent of the difference, is no democracy." There's an authoritarian strain in blue as well as red America. A thin line separates the will of the majority and the will to power. How many of us have enough self-restraint to keep the first from being corrupted by the second?

I don't mean that the majority shouldn't rule—it must. And I don't mean that the answer to our fathomless divide is to settle for an empty compromise at the midway point of every question. Centrism is a shortcut around hard judgments, leading to a dead end. But both secession and conquest abandon America to permanent polarization. Are we really there?

I want to resist and say: Not quite, not yet. The time of separation has given us a chance to look long and hard in the mirror, something Americans rarely do. I don't want to waste it. Before life starts up again, we have a moment to ask ourselves: With all our divisions, what do we have in common? Is there some underlying adhesive that can make us one country again? Can we still call all to the duty we owe to each?

For much of my life an idea persisted, here and abroad, for better and worse—that America was a kind of universal nation. It was the flip side of our "exceptionalism." To be global was to be Americanized, to be American was to be globalized. This explains why Americans take the attention of the world for granted and expect to encounter fluent speakers of American English everywhere. It's our birthright to assume that people in far-flung countries will be familiar with American personalities and events. After the election, foreign news organizations tracked the vote count hour by hour. I can't identify the prime minister of the Netherlands or Spain (can you?), but Dutch and Spanish people quickly learned the names of swing counties in Arizona and Georgia. "Know that who you vote for changes our lives!" an Iranian song-and-dance group pleaded with Americans in a music video. "Hey, Peter, Alice, look—our hands high in prayer! What's gonna happen in America?" A change of administration in Washington can send the price of beef soaring in Tehran.

This influence always went far beyond our ability to impose our will. It's strongest where no coercion is involved. Our culture has a pervasive reach beyond anything the British Empire or Soviet internationalism or the French *mission civilisatrice* achieved—this in spite of Americans' unwillingness to live abroad. Gilbert and Sullivan did not catch on in India (though cricket did), Ethiopian Marxists weren't converted to vodka and pirozhki, and a century of French culture in Indochina was overwhelmed by a few years of Motown and G.I. slang. The George Floyd protests in cities like Amsterdam and Tunis were a sign of American soft power. So was the presidency of Donald Trump—it encouraged populist demagogues on almost every continent.

Our culture doesn't have to be imposed at gunpoint or protected by a national academy. It spreads like a catchy tune that sticks in your mind against your will, which is why it has enraged generations of *philosophes* and clerics. Ours might be the only imperial culture that is resisted by local elites and adopted by ordinary people, not the other way around. In Ivory Coast, a former French colony with 40,000 French expats, young men in slums and villages style themselves after American gangsta rappers; so do Muslim boys who live in the housing projects surrounding Paris. Cheap, blatant, and readily accessible, American pop culture was made for the world's first leisured masses. It's almost designed to offend snobs, which is why *cultural* anti-Americanism tends to take root in the traditional upper ranks of societies. No working-class Englishman ever despised Americans as much as Graham Greene and John le Carré, both products of prep school, Oxford, and the British spy service. "I only have to see their Mormon haircuts and listen to their open-plan charm," le Carré wrote of his counterparts in the CIA. "I have only to hear them call Europe 'Yurrp' and I start sweating at the joints."

In Robert Stone's novel *A Flag for Sunrise*, an American anthropologist named Frank Holliwell, having consumed too much scotch and left his reading glasses in his hotel room, improvises an increasingly aggressive lecture to an audience at a Central American university. "In my country we have a saying—Mickey Mouse will see you dead," Holli-well announces. "There isn't really such a saying," he quickly admits. "I made it up to demonstrate, to dramatize the seriousness with which American popular culture should be regarded. Now American pop culture is often laughed at by snobbish foreigners—as we call them. But let me tell you that we have had the satisfaction of ramming it down their throats. These snobbish foreigners are going to learn to laugh around it or choke to death."

Foreigners didn't have to force down our way of life—they ate it up. I don't just mean our music, movies, food, clothes, sports, manners, and idioms. I mean that our system of political economy, democratic capitalism, which produced our mass culture, was also a universal model, especially after the fall of the Berlin Wall. Some yearned for it, some hated it, some tried to adopt it, but no one could be indifferent to it. While Michael Jordan, *Titanic*, and Microsoft held the world's attention, Americans never had to think about other countries—thus our notorious ignorance. Why should we know or care that Denmark votes by proportional representation? Other countries weren't real to us. We were the magnetic pole, and they would gravitate toward us or resist us, but their own particularities didn't interest us. Mickey Mouse would see them dead.

The idea that America is unique and superior among nations, exempt from the cruder forces of history, with a special mission to shine the light of liberty to the world—the idea that led to some of our noblest ventures and worst mistakes—has become impossible to sustain. A series of disasters, most of them self-inflicted, including Trump and the ravages of the pandemic, have thrown the shining city off its hill and down into the swarming world. Exceptional and Universal America finally ended in the early months of 2020, when the United States assumed (and would never relinquish) first place on the Coronavirus Worldometer, and Russia and Taiwan and the United Nations sent us humanitarian aid, and the world looked on in horror and pity.

It was the pity that did it. We really weren't doing so much worse than some others, but we were doing no better. Our quality of life placed us somewhere between Belgium and the United Arab Emirates. Natives of Iran and Bosnia warned their American-born friends how quickly everything could fall apart if we let Trump wreak much more havoc, and how many years or decades it could take to come back. In short, we were just one country among many, vulnerable to the same catastrophes as others, no exemptions granted. Big, rich, important, but nothing special. Certainly no longer a beacon of democracy. I have to admit—that hurt. What a comeuppance!

But it also has this benefit. It frees us to think about our country in a new way—not as a divine miracle or universal model, but as itself. Right when we're losing faith in anything like a shared identity, it allows us to look for one. Other countries have their particularities, their national traits that make them whole and distinct. So do we.

To generalize is to omit, distort, and probably offend.

It's risky. I'm sure you'll have no trouble coming up with instant exceptions and counterexamples. But please allow me to generalize about a continent-sized nation of 330 million crazily diverse and individualistic people anyway. An Amazon programmer is riding the G train to meet a Grindr date at a club in Williamsburg, a roofing contractor is fixing his carburetor on his driveway in Shreveport, a marine biologist is driving her daughter to field hockey practice in Santa Cruz, and an Iowa farm widow is canning blackberry jam for her church food pantry. What do they have in common? Nothing, of course. As soon as you try to see them as parts of a whole, all the particularities come flying at you.

But think a little more. There are certain markers that identify us as American. These are easier to pick up when Americans go abroad or foreigners come here—when we see ourselves in contrast. Some random observations: New York's subways are dirtier, its restaurants louder, and its taxis in worse repair than those in Toronto or Brussels. Public spaces in America are more squalid, there are more unrestrained displays of desire and frustration, and everything, from the cars to the servings of food, is bigger, including the people. For a rich country America is surprisingly poor, closer in ways to Brazil than to Canada, and Americans tolerate a level of poverty that people in countries with less wealth never would. "Tolerate" because its depth has no relation to gross domestic product. American poverty is a national choice.

There's more violence. We're famous for it. So many

evils in contemporary American life, from street crime, mass shootings, and police brutality to the barbarism of our prison system, have their origins in two features of U.S. history that left Europe behind: slavery and the frontier, the brutal control of one part of the population and the near-extermination of another. Road rage was invented here, not just because we live in our cars, but because the psychological cost of backing off is too high. I've seen traffic confrontations in many other countries, but they rarely escalate to American extremes. Other nationalities yell, gesticulate, mutter, and drive on, undiminished by what amounted to a ritual. Here, we go from zero to murder, just to avoid losing face—because it isn't a ritual, it's personal and directly threatens our need to be masters of ourselves. Which is why Americans, especially American men, are so easily humiliated. The daily affronts to equal status also explain why Americans murder one another in such large numbers. D. H. Lawrence wrote, in *Studies in Classic American Literature*, "The essential American soul is hard, isolate, stoic, and a killer." That is not the entire soul, but it's a recognizable part.

It's harder to explain why violence and kindness often come together. How many scenes in American movies begin with someone buying a round of drinks and end with the same man assaulting his new friends, or vice versa? Barack Obama, in his youthful autobiography *Dreams from My Father*, described the Kansas of his grandparents as a place where "decency" and "unblinking cruelty" were "joined at the hip." And no region is both friendlier and more violent than the South. During the war in Iraq, I noticed that U.S. soldiers tried to make friends with Iraqis in a way that occupying troops from other countries never did. They also turned to force much faster and harder, sometimes on a dime, in a way that Iraqis found terrifying and bewildering. An Iraqi prisoner would be beaten and kicked one minute and given excellent medical treatment the next. This double-faced quality is summed up in the motto of the Marine Corps: "No better friend, no worse enemy." It tells you something about a nation's character that its armed forces want to be seen that way. It's as if easy warmth and sudden violence are expressions of the same American informality, the lack of subtlety, the habit of taking action without much thought.

Violence, like music and so much else in American culture, is the inheritance of a history in which Black and white have lived forever in vexed proximity. We have never wanted to know just how inextricable we are, for we have never wanted to face this history—it contains too many devastating recognitions. Americans live in the future, not the past, which makes us childish to older nationalities. If 2020 is the year in which we finally stopped looking away from what white and Black people have done to each other and themselves during their four hundred years together in the New World, then it won't be a moment too soon, if it hasn't come too late.

But the generation that brings this reckoning is so obsessed with "difference" that it's forgotten or never knew what writers like Ralph Ellison, Zora Neale Hurston, Albert Murray, and (though he's no longer quoted for this) James Baldwin insisted on: Black culture *is* American culture, and American culture is Black culture. It's impossible to imagine one without the other. Murray, writing at the violent climax of the sixties and defying the "folklore" of white supremacy, called us "omni-Americans": products of a culture that is "*patently and irrevocably composite . . . incontestably mulatto.* Indeed, for all their traditional antagonisms and obvious differences, the so-called black and so-called white people of the United States resemble nobody else in the world so much as they resemble each other."

After exiling himself in Paris to escape the American prison house of race, Baldwin made the same discovery: "I proved, to my astonishment, to be as American as any Texas G.I. And I found my experience was shared by every American writer I knew in Paris. Like me, they had been divorced from their origins, and it turned out to make very little difference that the origins of white Americans were European and mine were African—they were no more at home in Europe than I was." In dense, settled Europe Baldwin found his great subject—his own country, "in which nothing is fixed and in which the individual must fight for his identity."

We carry the marks of our birth with us throughout our lives. The very effort to escape them shows their indelibility. But we see them most clearly through the eyes of others. What do foreigners say about us? Exactly what we notice in our compatriots when we encounter them abroad, cringe, and head the other way, because we recognize ourselves. That we speak in loud voices, that we smile a lot, that we immediately use first names, that the answer to how we're doing is always "Great," that we make friends easily and have no secrets but the intimacies are shallow and ephemeral, that we have no talent and little interest in foreign languages, that we think too much about money, that we lack a tragic sense, that we're admirably practical and annoyingly moralistic, that we can't see shades of gray, only black and white. They find us open, direct, arrogant, and naïve.

Most of these qualities suggest that Americans don't take national differences very seriously. We imagine that, just below the surface, we're all basically the same—a humane assumption that has led us into our stupidest wars. Americans in foreign countries are vaguely aware that we are constantly violating subtle but important codes—that intricate layers of history and social relations determine who should take an empty seat or whether an invitation is sincere. The Iranian concept of *taarof*—a complex etiquette of civility determined by deference to social rank—is as incomprehensible to an American as Sanskrit. Indirection is alien to us—we find it baffling, phony, a waste of time—which is why Americans have trouble living in countries where codes of behavior are compiled and refined through centuries. When foreigners come here, the social landscape lies before them flat and featureless. They might encounter ugly prejudice, but they won't need to learn how many times it's proper to refuse before accepting their host's offer of seconds.

Related to this unsubtlety is our lack of gravity—the disregard for limits and sense of eternal possibility in new things. We untether, flit, and make ourselves over as if nothing is too fixed or solid for change. We are world-class inventors, especially of ourselves. At the same time, we take pride in ordinariness and are suspicious of airs, especially intellectual ones. Anti-intellectualism, Richard Hofstadter wrote in his study of the subject, has been a defining American trait from the Puritan beginnings: "It made its way into our politics because it became associated with our passion for equality."

That passion explains almost every generalization I've made here. Equality is the hidden American code, the unspoken feeling that everyone shares, even if it's not articulated or fulfilled: the desire to be everyone's equal—which is not the same thing as the desire for everyone to be equal. Equality is the first truth of our founding document, the one that leads to all the others. The word of the eighteenth-century Declaration became flesh in the dynamic commercial society of the nineteenth. Tocqueville described equality as the "ardent, insatiable, eternal, and invincible" desire of democratic peoples. A few years later, in *Leaves of Grass*, Whitman conveyed this desire as a secular religion:

> *He says indifferently and alike* How are you friend? *to the*
> *President at his levee,*
> *And he says* Good-day my brother, *to Cudge that hoes in*
> *the sugar-field,*
> *And both understand him and know that his speech is right.*

He walks with perfect ease in the capitol,
He walks among the Congress, and one Representative says to
    another, Here is our equal appearing and new.

The code of equality shapes so many things in American life. It helps to explain our reputation for being blunt and clueless, the innocence about other ways of life that leads civilized foreigners to despise us. Our instinctive egalitarianism makes us poor interpreters of the mores of different stations and classes. It's why we have no formal address, why American waiters are breezy—"Hi, my name's Justin and I'll be taking care of you tonight"—in a way that would offend the dignity of restaurant staff in just about any other country. Most other democracies have roots in feudalism, blood, and soil. The intricacies of rank and ties still shape their cultures. For several centuries America has absorbed people from all over the world into a culture that's blatant and accessible enough to provide a lingua franca in which they can understand and be understood without too much pain, and that's malleable enough for them to shape in their turn.

The most widely read classics of American literature are stories of individual striving and defeat with little broader context. Even a novel like Richard Wright's *Native Son*, a work of intense political criticism, gives a crude picture of society compared with what you would find in a European social novel—it's the story of Bigger Thomas against the world. The least American novel I've ever read is *The Remains of the Day*, by Kazuo Ishiguro, who is British of

Japanese origin, about an English butler whose sense of so-cial position makes personal fulfillment impossible.

We accept terrible poverty because we believe, despite a mountain of evidence to the contrary, in fluid social mobil-ity. The myth of the self-made man and equal opportunity—never entirely wrong—lets us live with extreme inequalities of result. The vast majority of Americans describe them-selves as middle class, even if their incomes and educations put them in the top or bottom 10 percent. A people who can't shut up about identity don't like to talk about class at all. Many books have asked why there is no socialism in the United States and arrived at many different answers, but the most convincing, paradoxically, is our passion for equality.

It also explains why the South has always seemed alien to the rest of the country: not because of racism, which is nationwide, but because of the feudal dreams that slavery made possible. Only in the South has aristocracy been held up as a cherished collective ideal rather than privately pur-sued as an enviable state. One of the great works of Ameri-can sociology, *The Mind of the South* by W. J. Cash, called its subject "not quite a nation within a nation, but the next thing to it." And yet many of the characteristics that Cash found in his home region—"an inclination to act from feel-ing rather than from thought, an exaggerated individual-ism and a too narrow concept of social responsibility"—are recognizably American, showing the country's wholeness through even its least digestible part.

The code always made one exception. The perpetual test of equality in America is the condition of Black Americans. This was what Ralph Ellison meant when he said, "In the United States the Negro and his status have always stood for that moral concern. He symbolizes among other things the human and social possibility of equality." There are countries where a minority group can be relegated permanently to an inferior status without generating endless social conflict, but not here. When our code is broken, our democratic system will eventually break down, too. "Of all dangers to a nation, as things exist in our day," Whitman wrote in *Democratic Vistas*, "there can be no greater one than having certain portions of the people set off from the rest by a line drawn—they not privileged as others, but degraded, humiliated, made of no account." If equality isn't possible for Black Americans, it isn't possible for America.

The great danger of equality is atomization. If we're all side by side on the same level and constantly in motion, there's no fixed relation between us. "Aristocracy links everybody, from peasant to king, in one long chain," Tocqueville wrote. "Democracy breaks the chain and frees each link." Equal and independent people will satisfy their own desires with no obligation to others outside their narrow circle. The chance to be anything or anyone gives them the idea that they don't owe anything to anyone. They grow indifferent to the common good and withdraw from others into the pursuit of personal happiness, especially wealth. Tocqueville called this "individualism." It explains how the American passion for equality can lead to extreme inequality, even a new aristocracy, but one without links between people.

The solution for individualism is not religion or human fellowship or central planning—it's self-government, which allows us to work through free institutions for a common purpose. "The Americans have used liberty to combat the individualism born of equality, and they have won," Tocqueville declared. But when equality disappears, there's no longer any basis for shared citizenship, the art of self-government is lost, and everything falls apart. This is our condition today. Democracy is not just parchment and marble, the Constitution, rights, laws, and institutions. It's also the action that can bring us out of our isolation and bind us together. But we cannot act as fellow citizens unless we are equal.

At the start of World War II, George Orwell described England as "a family with the wrong members in control." No one except a politician would call America a family. Mario Cuomo did it in a magnificent speech at the Democratic convention in 1984, and that year his party was wiped out. There are too many of us, we're too scattered, and we don't have the shared memories and in-jokes of blood relatives. Instead of a family tree there's a wilderness. But we are connected, whether or not we want to be.

Rather than a family, with its involuntary intimacy, we're like strangers who have come to do separate things together—like people at a fair. There are rides, booths, games, and freaks. There's a bandstand, a chapel, and a strip show. Markets hawk every imaginable product, and the din of buying and selling is deafening. The crowd is a herd of in-dividuals, but there are unwritten rules that everyone un-derstands. Once or twice a day the bedlam pauses, all turn their attention to the main event, and a thrilling bond passes through them to be doing the same thing together. There's also a current of suspicion, because someone is always about to get scammed. When a fight breaks out, and fights often do, the fairgoers have to settle it among themselves. They have to clean the alleys and restock the stalls and repair the platforms. There's no higher authority in charge. The fair belongs to them.

National characteristics don't create national unity. Civil wars have been fought in countries with a common culture, including ours. The qualities I've sketched out—you might have others to add or put in their place—don't make us a nation. They just show the contours of concealed ligaments that would be torn if we continue pulling apart.

The year 2020 felt like a mode of living played out. Every shock set off an alarm for radical change in our relations to one another, our economy, our government, and the world. But countries are not social science experiments. They have organic qualities, some positive, some destructive, that can't be wished away. Knowing who we are lets us see what kinds of change are possible. The past doesn't tell us what will happen next, but it suggests what we can and cannot be-come. The desire to be equal, the individualism it produces, the hustle for money, the love of novelty, the attachment to democracy, the distrust of authority and intellect—these won't disappear. A way forward that tries to evade or crush them on the road to some free, smart, real, or just utopia will never arrive and instead will run into a strong reaction. But a way forward that tries to make us equal citizens, free to shape our shared destiny, is a road that connects our past and our future.

EQUALIZERS

I n 1853 *The New York Times* published an article by Julia Tyler, second wife of the tenth president, replying to an anti-slavery petition organized by a group of titled British women. The former first lady, a northerner by birth, was living on her husband's Virginia plantation with around sixty enslaved people at her disposal. Sounding like Tocqueville at his most enthusiastic, she described to her aristocratic "English sisters" the limitless possibilities of American democracy: "a free, prosperous, and great people, among whom all artificial distinctions of society are unknown; where preferment is equally open to all, and man's capacity for self-government is recognized and conclusively established." Mrs. Tyler then turned on a scornful display of whataboutism: What about the British slave trade? What about the West Indies? The starving Irish? The British working class? "The negro of the South lives sumptuously in comparison with the 100,000 of the white population in London. He is clothed well in Winter, and has his meat twice daily, without stint of bread." The British ladies should mind their own business.

The rival paper to the more elite *Times* was *The New York Tribune*, a popular broadsheet edited by Horace Greeley, an idiosyncratic genius from Nowheresville. Greeley saw an opportunity to stick it to the Slave Power as well as to the competition. Several months later, the *Tribune* published a reply to the former first lady—a letter from a fugitive slave from North Carolina named Harriet Jacobs. Disguising herself as a "sister," she told a harrowing story of little children taken away from their mothers, of a teenage girl coerced by her owner, of "a miserable existence of two years, between the fires of her mistress's jealousy and her master's brutal passion." In her early twenties Jacobs fled; she then hid for seven years in a crawl space so small that she couldn't stand up, before finally escaping to the North, where she joined white and Black abolitionists. She ended the letter with a reference to Harriet Beecher Stowe: "Would that I had one spark from her store house of genius and talent, I would tell you of my own sufferings—I would tell you of wrongs that Hungary has never inflicted, nor England ever dreamed of in this free country where all nations fly for liberty, equal rights and protection under your stripes and stars. It should be stripes and scars, for they go along with Mrs. Tyler's peculiar circumstances."

The letter was Jacobs's first effort at what would turn into one of the essential narratives of American slavery. Greeley published it as a small firebomb in the escalating war for public opinion during the decade leading to the Civil War. Southerners tried to destroy copies of the *Tribune* with Jacobs's letter before they could reach readers.

These years we're living through feel like the 1850s—one crisis after another, an impending collapse that keeps being postponed, an unbearable tension between mutual hatred and inconceivable disunion. There have been several near-death experiences in American history: the Gilded Age, the Great Depression, the Sixties, and the nearest of all, the Civil War. Each of them was in some way brought on by inequality, the broken American code, none starker than that between citizen and slave. We're living through one of our own. It throws up different problems and makes different demands, but nothing is really new. Earlier Americans used the same tools of citizenship that are in our possession—journalism, government, activism—when they thought democracy was about to commit suicide. They show us ways of being American that we've forgotten—that can fortify and instruct us in our own crisis.

The worst one in American history was also a crisis within Horace Greeley. Even more than Lincoln, Greeley was a fervent opponent of slavery, and he used the mass media of his day to bring national passions to the boiling point. But when the war came, the failure of the national experiment nearly broke him.

In almost every way Greeley's life defied the categories in which we're used to thinking. He was a kind of American and a kind of journalist who no longer make sense. He combined elements of all four narratives and moved through their spheres without encountering high walls. America in the first half of the nineteenth century was, for white men, a far more fluid, less hierarchical country than the one we live in, and if there was ever a self-made man, it was Greeley. He was a son of the obscure rural poor of Real America, born in 1811 to New England farmers. He was largely self-educated in small-town libraries of New Hampshire and Vermont, and as a young man he walked literally hundreds of miles to get where he needed to go. He respected learning, but not, he said, if it was merely "directed to the acquisition of wealth and luxury by means which add little to the aggregate of human comforts." He didn't mistake talent for Smart America's system of institutional credentialing. There was no contradiction for Greeley between rootedness and ambition, attachment to the soil and openness to innovation.

He arrived in New York City at age twenty to seek his fortune as an apprentice printer. Soon he became an entrepreneur, starting a series of papers that each failed, before he founded the *Tribune* in 1841. By 1860 it was the most widely read newspaper in the world and Greeley was the most important journalist in America, but his target audiences were urban workers, many of them Irish and German immigrants, and the growing farm communities of the Midwest. He never stopped identifying with working men and women, remaining a member of the printers' union at the paper he owned. He was on familiar terms with the great men of his day, including Lincoln, but he dressed like an eccentric tramp in baggy clothes under an old Irish linen coat.

For Greeley, equality meant the chance for all people to rise and make themselves virtuous citizens, and journalism was essential to this project. His *Tribune*, though populist, was not the clickbait of its time. He wanted to elevate his readers with political debate, philosophy, literature, and news. He was a partisan editor—a Whig until the party collapsed in the 1850s, then a founder of its successor, the Republican Party—but he published Henry David Thoreau, Karl Marx, the feminist Margaret Fuller, and the utopian socialist Albert Brisbane, and he quarreled with all of them. He didn't fear being in the minority or the wrong, and partisanship didn't make him want to silence the other side.

Greeley was in constant motion in pursuit of the public good; as for self-interest, he was forever in debt. His rival William Seward said, "What can you do with a man of sixty ideas, and every one of the sixty an impracticable crochet?" Greeley wanted to fire his readers with zeal for the various reform causes that consumed him—temperance, cooperative communities, homesteading ("Go West, young man"), and above all anti-slavery. For Greeley a free press was as essential to human happiness as free labor. It was not just a constitutional right, but a weapon against the Slave Power. Free speech was on the side of Just America. Only the South, through laws and violence, tried to crush it.

For the first part of his career, Greeley regarded slavery mainly as a threat to free labor in the North. He was not an abolitionist—hardly any white person was. Like Lincoln, he advocated colonization of freed slaves in Africa. Then, in 1837, an abolitionist Congregational minister and newspaper editor named Arthur Lovejoy was shot to death in Alton, Illinois, by a pro-slavery mob that destroyed his printing press. This murder propelled young Lincoln, two months later in nearby Springfield, to give the speech in which he proclaimed, "As a nation of freemen, we must live through all time, or die by suicide." The incident had an even more decisive effect on young Greeley. "If I had ever been one of those who sneeringly asked, 'What have we of the North to do with Slavery?' the murder of Lovejoy would have supplied me with a conclusive answer," he wrote in his memoirs. "It was thenceforth plain to my apprehension, that Slavery and true Freedom could not coexist on the same soil."

Greeley came to believe that civil war was inevitable. After the Kansas-Nebraska Act of 1854, which permitted the extension of slavery into western territories, he did his best to bring it about. America was in the midst of what the historian Daniel Walker Howe calls a "communications revolution": the telegraph, the steam-powered rotary press, and the railroad made local news almost immediately national, and slavery an inescapably national issue. In the propaganda war that preceded the war itself, an editor like Greeley was as powerful as any politician. When the new territory became an actual battleground, "Bleeding Kansas," he inflamed northern readers with the *Tribune* correspondent's lurid stories of the slavers' violence (not hesitating to downplay the counterviolence of John Brown and his militia), and even raised money to send anti-slavery emigrants to Kansas. The *Tribune* also hyped the violence in Congress, where representatives began showing up to work armed and regularly threatened and beat one another. Greeley himself was punched in the head and caned near the Capitol by a drunken Arkansas congressman whom the *Tribune* had attacked. John Brown's raid on Harpers Ferry in 1859 and subsequent hanging made Brown a martyr in Greeley's pages. An Alabama paper called for Greeley to be executed, or sent to a desert island where wild animals would devour him.

After doing so much to bring the country to the verge of war, he was unhinged by its arrival. Lincoln and Greeley were both nationalists, but where Lincoln viewed the war as essential to the survival of self-government, Greeley feared that the fighting would destroy it. This conflict between national unity and equality for all citizens plagued Greeley for the rest of his days, and he found increasingly perverse ways to resolve it. At first he wanted to let the South go its own way; soon he reversed himself. He was ready to surrender in 1861 after the disaster at Bull Run drove him to a nervous breakdown. In 1862, appalled that the slaughter served no higher purpose than coercing the Confederacy back into the Union, he publicly urged Lincoln to free all slaves. In 1864 he tried to negotiate peace with southern agents. After the war, he advocated the franchise for freed slaves but also amnesty for Jefferson Davis and other Confederates. In 1872

Greeley ran against President Grant as a "Liberal Republican" on a platform of reconciliation with the South and an end to Reconstruction. Even with the endorsement of the Democratic Party, he lost in a landslide and died a few weeks later. At his funeral in Manhattan, 40,000 working men and women, white and Black, paid their respects.

At the end of his life Greeley didn't realize that the country he had grown up in, of self-made men free to rise through their own labor, no longer existed. The triumph of the Union and the end of slavery did not lead to the virtuous republic of equal citizens that Greeley imagined. America was entering an age of monopoly, class conflict, and white redemption. Like most of us, he outlived his understanding of the world. What we should remember from Greeley's life is not any particular view or enthusiasm, but the kind of American it was possible to be: an extraordinary man who never stopped identifying with ordinary people; a journalist whose vocation was to be a citizen.

Frances Perkins was as woke as any social justice warrior. Her story shows us a way to be woke that we need to remember if we hope to do half as much for social justice as her generation achieved.

The Progressives grew up in a world whose scale and complexity the Civil War generation of Lincoln and Greeley and Whitman had never dreamed of. They were mostly middle-class Protestants, as anxious about their status as today's professionals. They had their eyes opened in the Gilded Age to the shame of the slums and the tyranny of the trusts—another version of suicide for a self-governing republic. They were thrown into the urban industrial twentieth century as unready as we've been thrown into the networked digital twenty-first. Around the turn of the century they underwent a collective moral awakening of the kind that occasionally seizes comfortable Americans and can resemble religious feeling. The awakening produced a new culture of literature, art, and journalism that dramatized the horror of factories and tenements.

The Progressives were inspired and frightened by movements from below among farmers and workers, and they set out to realize the reform ideas of the Populists and Socialists through democratic institutions. The ills that concerned them were the same as ours: monopoly and corruption, poverty and inequality, the problems of mass immigration and rapid technological change, the rights of women. Only racial injustice was not on their agenda. Most Black people still lived in the South, where, after Reconstruction's tragic demise, they had fallen under the long night of Jim Crow.

Perkins was a middle-class girl, born in Massachusetts in 1880, educated at Mount Holyoke. She had her awakening in college, as usual. An economic history professor (a woman—all her early mentors were women) sent her students to local factories, where they interviewed workers on their conditions, and this, along with reading *How the Other Half Lives*, Jacob Riis's documentary of the Lower East Side, was Perkins's conversion experience. So she set out to be a social worker.

That was no easy thing for a respectable young woman in 1902. Her parents expected her to marry after graduation and join society. Perkins fled to Chicago, where she took a job teaching in a girls' school. But she soon found her way to Hull House, Jane Addams's pioneering settlement house in the Near West Side ghetto, where middle-class activists provided essential services to the urban destitute while sharing meals and arranging performances, debates, and lectures in a genuine community, free of what Addams called "professional doing good." Half a century later, here was the same egalitarian spirit of self-improvement and social reform, rooted in democracy and Christianity, that animated Greeley and his *Tribune*. It runs like a bright thread through American history.

Perkins had no intellectual apparatus, no arcane language, for explaining poverty, and this innocence, particular to her time, was a great advantage over our labyrinths of knowing theories. Instead of expertise she had confidence. "Social work was so new, so undefined, that almost any energetic young person of goodwill could pitch in and do what seemed best," she said years later. "There weren't any principles. I didn't have any training." She was simply moved to object to suffering and injustice, a response that never deserted her and gave her the means to remake her America.

We no longer use the Progressives' moral language—it embarrasses us, it sounds naïve. Instead of "wrong" and "unjust"

we say "problematic" and "marginalizing," words that turn social justice into specialized work and warn everyone else off,
while raising a barrier between thought and action. A condition for action is the clarity of mind that lets you believe you
can and must act, and the inspiration of a positive vision. If
any idea animated Perkins and her peers, it was, she said, "the
idea that poverty is preventable, that poverty is destructive,
wasteful, demoralizing, and that poverty in the midst of potential plenty is morally unacceptable in a Christian and democratic society. One began to see the 'poor' as people, with
hopes, fears, virtues, and vices, as fellow citizens who were
part of the fabric of American life instead of as a depressed
class who would be always with us." This consciousness was,
to Perkins, a form of "patriotism based upon the love of the
men and women who were fellow citizens." A century ago, to
be woke was to be patriotic.

Perkins returned east and ended up in New York, where
she did graduate work at Columbia and then, in 1909,
took a job with the National Consumers League, which
advocated for rights and protections for workers, especially
women and children. Unions and the immigrants they organized terrified prosperous native-born Americans, but Perkins, through innumerable visits to sweatshops, began to see
labor as a powerful, if narrow and self-interested, tool for
reform. She also had a talent for making connections with
important people—the philosopher John Dewey and the
novelist Upton Sinclair in Chicago, Upper East Side philan-
thropists and Greenwich Village radicals and artists in New

York. She was able to move between the worlds of the elites and the masses in a way that seems unthinkable today.

Her life's turning point came on March 25, 1911. That afternoon she was having tea with a wealthy friend whose windows looked out on Washington Square. The noise of shouting and sirens rose from the street, and a butler came in to report a large fire across the park. Perkins rushed outside and saw flames consuming the upper floors of a ten-story building where the Triangle Shirtwaist Company had a factory. Perkins knew the place. Italian and Jewish seamstresses, most in their teens and twenties, had gone on strike to bring changes to working conditions there, including improved fire safety; they'd been beaten and jailed, the effort had failed, and exit doors in the sweatshop remained locked to prevent theft or unauthorized breaks. As Perkins approached through a frenzied crowd, she saw girls, women, and men hanging out the high windows, falling or jumping to their death on the street below. Altogether, 146 people died in the fire that day. Perkins later called it "the day the New Deal began."

The horror she witnessed turned Perkins to a wider arena of activism—politics. The ills of industrial capitalism would never be solved by the private efforts of social workers and labor groups alone. The former president Theodore Roosevelt made her executive secretary of the state's new Committee on Safety, and Perkins began to lobby officials in Albany for reforms, starting with fire safety measures and a 54-hour workweek for women—the first labor laws of their type anywhere in the United States. Politics required new skills that asked more of her than personal morality. She was up against machine politicians and the corporations that owned them, and she learned how to mobilize influential supporters and win over dubious, sometimes corrupt allies; when to push harder and when to compromise; and how to disarm macho, suspicious labor leaders with her knowledge and empathy. She figured out how to ingratiate herself with powerful politicians by dressing and behaving so that "you remind them subconsciously of their mothers." She became indispensable to Al Smith, and after he was elected governor of New York in 1918 he brought her into state government with a seat on his industrial board, making Perkins the highest-paid female official in America, just as women's suffrage was being ratified to the Constitution.

After Franklin Roosevelt replaced Smith in 1929, he made Perkins his industrial commissioner. Almost immediately, the worst economic collapse in American history gave her the chance to put years of experience into radical action with the country's first unemployment insurance system. When Roosevelt was elected president in 1932, he summoned Perkins to his town house on East Sixty-fifth Street and offered her the position of secretary of labor, which would make her the first ever woman cabinet member.

She had come armed with a list of programs, reforms that she had been pursuing for years on the city and state levels. The list would be her condition for accepting the offer: federal jobless relief and unemployment insurance, public works, old-age pensions, minimum wage and maximum hours, a ban on child labor. She had about half the New Deal in her pocket, and Roosevelt cheerfully accepted. "I suppose you are going to nag me about this forever," he said as she got up to leave. She had a deep understanding of FDR, and she knew that he wanted her to keep his conscience.

Perkins, age fifty-two, became secretary of labor at the depth of the Great Depression. Only an activist national government could hold off economic catastrophe and perhaps the end of democracy. One of her first meetings was with coal operators so desperate for help that they begged the federal government to buy their mines at any price. "I suddenly got the sense of responsibility to a whole industry and to a whole nation and not merely to the President or to my special field," she later wrote. "I had a sense of what 'the Government of the United States,' put into just those words, means in its influence, leadership, and conscience for all the people of the United States."

Perkins spent the twelve years of Roosevelt's presidency doing more than anyone other than FDR himself to make the New Deal a reality. Everything on her list became law, most notably social security, changing the basic relation of Americans to their government. She also desegregated the Labor Department cafeteria, tried (and failed) to bring large numbers of Jewish refugees from Hitler into the country, survived a congressional impeachment effort, and endured endless insults in the press. If her story isn't familiar to you, perhaps it's because she had to be careful not to overshadow the men.

The New Deal wasn't just a set of radically new government programs. It was a patriotic mythology that drew on earlier American myths, placing the ordinary citizen, the "forgotten man at the bottom of the economic pyramid," again at the center of a great national project. Langston Hughes captured the idea in his poem "Let America Be America Again," written in 1935 on an all-night train ride:

> *O, yes,*
> *I say it plain,*
> *America never was America to me,*
> *And yet I swear this oath—*
> *America will be!*

Six years later, in 1941, the Black labor leader A. Philip Randolph announced plans for a march on Washington to demand integration of the armed forces. FDR met with Randolph but was unable to get him to call it off. So the rattled president issued an executive order banning discrimination in the federal government and the defense industry. This was enough for Randolph to cancel the march, but his young lieutenant, a twenty-nine-year-old pacifist named Bayard Rustin—raised by Quaker grandparents outside

Philadelphia—vehemently objected. The military would remain segregated throughout the war. Later in life Rustin became known in left-wing circles as a moderate, even a conservative. Today, in Just America, nonviolence is often considered a form of weakness and accommodation. In fact, Rustin was as radical as anyone, in belief as well as action. His honesty and independence made him a frequent target from all sides at a time when there was no forgiveness for apostasy, just like today.

If Perkins, the Progressive turned New Dealer, spent her life addressing problems left behind by Greeley's Civil War generation—corporate power, exploited labor, political corruption, poverty—Rustin spent his battling injustices that the New Deal generation didn't address: racism, segregation, and the threat of militarism to world peace. No one in the Black freedom struggle, with the exception of Martin Luther King, Jr., was more important than Rustin, but he was the movement's lone rider. He worked in a wide array of left organizations—Christian, pacifist, labor, civil rights, human rights, socialist, even Communist when he was young—but he remained an outsider in all of them. "I did not consider myself a leader," he once said—he was a strategist and planner. He was also gay, and this made him a pariah even to his own comrades, forcing him into the shadows whenever his profile grew too big.

Rustin was tall and slender, wore his hair long, and spoke with a mandarin accent. No one who met him could come away without respect. During World War II he spent twenty-eight months in a federal prison in Kentucky as a conscientious objector. In 1949 he was sentenced to thirty days on a North Carolina chain gang for sitting in a white seat on an interstate bus—a Freedom Rider years before they became famous in 1961. He organized his fellow prisoners to demand better conditions, while treating his jailers with such courtesy ("without losing one's self-respect or submitting completely to outside authority") that they came to depend on this "agitator." As a militant of nonviolence Rustin endured numerous beatings and was arrested twenty-four times—twenty-three for acts of civil disobedience and one, in Pasadena in 1953, for "lewd vagrancy." That was the one that haunted him.

In early 1956 Rustin traveled to Montgomery, Alabama, as an emissary of northern activists to the leaders of the bus boycott, then two months old. White supremacists had bombed the house of the young Baptist minister who was the boycott's spokesman, and the activists were concerned that the boycott might turn to violence. At that point King knew little about Gandhian philosophy, let alone how to apply it in the intense heat of direct action. Rustin urged King to get rid of the guns in his house and disarm his bodyguards, and when the boycott's leaders faced mass arrests he told them to show up in court dressed as if for church rather than waiting shame-faced at home to be brought in—jail for their beliefs should be a source of pride. Rustin quickly became King's strategic advisor, as well as his connection to northern supporters. "I think he needed someone to talk to," Rustin recalled. "I think he totally depended on me, not that I was always right, but I would tell him the truth." More than anyone, Rustin infused the new movement with the ideas and tactics of nonviolence—he once called it "a moral jujitsu." He placed civil rights in the context of the larger cause of social justice in America and struggles worldwide for human rights and against colonialism.

Rustin remained at King's side in the early years of the Southern Christian Leadership Conference. Then, in 1960, their relationship was broken. The Harlem congressman Adam Clayton Powell, who saw in King a rival for Black leadership, told King that unless he called off a march on that summer's Democratic convention, which Powell took as encroachment on his turf, he would claim (falsely) that King and Rustin were having an affair. Rustin's homosexuality was an open secret; along with his brief membership in a Communist youth group in the thirties, it gave his enemies an eternal sword to hold over his head. King's courage did not extend as far as his sexual reputation. Rustin offered to resign, and he was devastated when King agreed. He never fully trusted King again.

Rustin's exile from the movement lasted several years. At the end of 1962, he and his mentor A. Philip Randolph, now an old man, discussed the idea of completing in 1963 what they had started and abandoned in 1941—a mass march on Washington, a hundred years after the Emancipation Proclamation with all its unfulfilled promise. Randolph and Rustin, socialists from the New Deal era, realized that the civil rights phase of the movement was approaching an end. The march would culminate that phase and begin a new one, based on social and economic issues—jobs, housing, health care, education—that applied to all Americans, white and Black. For this reason the march would have to be not just massive but also thoroughly integrated, with support from labor, clergy, and politicians, and it would be called the March on Washington for Jobs and Freedom. To the displeasure of other civil rights leaders, Randolph put Rustin in command of organizing it.

He was deep in the logistical details of buses and toilets when his sexual identity nearly destroyed him again. In mid-August 1963 J. Edgar Hoover's FBI passed its file on Rustin to Senator Strom Thurmond, the South Carolina segregationist. Thurmond gave a speech in Congress denouncing the Communist draft-dodging pervert in charge of the march, with details of the Pasadena arrest. Now the march itself was at stake, and this time the other civil rights leaders, led by Randolph and including King, rallied behind Rustin, who sent a statement to the press: "I am not the first of my race to have been falsely attacked by spokesmen of the Confederacy."

On August 28, 1963, Rustin stood on the steps of the Lincoln Memorial right by King's side throughout the "I Have a Dream" speech, arms tensely folded across his chest as if he didn't dare to relax until the last words were spoken, "Free at last, free at last, thank God almighty, we are free at last!" Then Rustin exploded in shouts and applause along with the quarter million people he had brought to the March on Washington.

At the end of the day, after the last discarded cup and scrap of paper on the National Mall had been picked up, he went to congratulate Randolph. "The greatest moment of my life was when I saw tears roll down the face of A. Philip Randolph," he later said. "To me he was the giant, and to see this giant with tears in his eyes moved me to want to do everything I humanly could do to bring about justice, not only for Black people but for whoever is in trouble."

The march that was Rustin's great achievement was also his political turning point. After the passage of the Civil Rights Act of 1964 he wrote an essay called "From Protest to Politics," published in *Commentary*. It argued that the battle for legal equality for Black people was largely over, and that the movement "is now concerned not merely with removing the barriers to full *opportunity* but with achieving the fact of *equality*." The implications of this new phase were profound. Gaining equal rights, including the right to vote, meant that the movement needed to leave the streets and enter rooms where decisions are made by people with power. It needed to enter politics, including the politics of building coalitions with other factions inside the Democratic Party—especially white liberals, labor, and Jews.

This change did not mean moderating goals—the opposite. Economic equality, lifting up poor Americans both white and Black, would require a far more dramatic transformation than simply getting rid of Jim Crow laws: "I believe that the Negro's struggle for equality in America is essentially revolutionary. While most Negroes—in their hearts—unquestionably seek only to enjoy the fruits of American society as it now exists, their quest cannot *objectively* be satisfied within the framework of existing political and economic relations."

This turn created strains between Rustin and his movement comrades, though King gradually came to embrace his view. It also made Rustin an enemy in the eyes of the New Left, white and Black, which torched him for selling out. Rustin returned the scorn. He saw Black Power as philosophically wrong and politically fatal—certain to drive away Americans whose support was essential for the kind of massive federal spending Rustin believed necessary to achieve "the fact of equality." The turn to political economy required the goals to be more ambitious but the tactics more restrained. The riots of the mid to late sixties and the threat of backlash made both needs more urgent (Rustin went to the burned-out streets of New York and Los Angeles to urge nonviolence, but now no one listened). He deplored the growing cultural separatism. "I am very much opposed to separatism under any circumstances and I'm also opposed to black studies," he wrote. He thought that it would ghettoize Black students, depriving them of the education they badly needed for real equality. Black history should be taught at the heart of American history. "In this country, to try to separate the Black experience from the American experience is ridiculous," Rustin wrote in the same vein as Albert Murray's *Omni-Americans*. He blamed self-flagellating liberals, nihilistic radicals, and a minority of militants who claimed to speak for the majority of Black people for taking up the racist notion of "the undifferentiated black community"—a lie that would only leave Black people powerless.

America was undergoing another near-death experience, and Rustin's rescue effort drove him into a series of doomed positions. His fear of alienating white allies led him into a perverse embrace of the Johnson administration at the height of the Vietnam War, which he made a determined effort to ignore. White Americans were not about to support a huge expansion of the Great Society, which the war was destroying. They were about to elect Richard Nixon, with a large minority for George Wallace. The 1968 election gave young militants the same bragging rights over Rustin that Trump gave Black Lives Matter activists over Obama in 2016. Equality is a lie. It's always been a lie, it will always be a lie.

Rustin never stopped his activism. He took up the cause of refugees in Southeast Asia and human rights in Poland. He defended Israel from anti-Zionists, appalling his left-wing friends. In the 1980s, in his seventies, he finally came out, free at last to live openly with a partner for the first time and speak on behalf of gay rights. He died in 1987, but it took another twenty-six years for him to receive his due, when President Obama bestowed the Medal of Freedom on the late Bayard Rustin.

MAKE AMERICA AGAIN

We've been here before. These stories should sound familiar: a house divided, monopoly and corruption, fixed classes of rich and poor, racial injustice. Greeley, Perkins, and Rustin faced versions of the same American trouble that we face: *Inequality destroys the sense of shared citizenship, and with it self-government.* We are becoming an aristocracy, and an ungovernable one. We could give the experts more power to govern us better, but then we would become even less capable of governing ourselves and end up under the rule of another demagogue. We've allowed things to drift this way for a long time, and now we hear the roar of the cataract. The task of bringing ourselves back from the edge is even harder than you might think.

It's common these days to hear people talk about sick America, dying America, the end of America. The thought has crossed my mind more than once. The same kinds of things were said in 1861, in 1893, in 1933, and in 1968.

The sickness, the death, is always a moral condition. Maybe this comes from our Puritan heritage. If we are dying, it can't be from natural causes. It must be a prolonged act of suicide, which is a form of murder.

Do other people personify their countries like that? If not, if it's another American quirk, then the reason might be that a country rooted in blood and soil doesn't die. Its culture can turn rotten, its economy collapse, its government fall to enemies foreign or domestic, but the nation will continue on in some bent and ragged shape while there's still blood and soil to nourish it. But a country based on a fervid and tremendous idea can die, and die pretty easily. It's as fragile as thought, as faith.

I don't think we are dying.

No other people in this era of elected authoritarians have been able to get rid of theirs—only Americans. Around the world they were paying attention and took hope. I hate that 74 million of my compatriots voted to keep in power our worst president, who convinced most of them that the election was stolen. The stab in the back will fester in their minds for years, a threat to the rest of us. But it's too easy to be riveted to that disturbing number and forget the 81 million who voted him out. It's too easy altogether to be riveted to chaos, vulgarity, and hatred, and I worry that we will be a while missing him for the sick anxious pleasure of watching what he does next. We will require a period of detoxification—stay hydrated, move carefully in case of vertigo or organ damage.

But I want to keep in mind the 81 million, and the poll workers, election officials, secretaries of state, judges, and reporters who exhibited civic virtue by simply doing their jobs.

Most of us still want our democracy. This is one lesson from the nightmare we've been through. We learned how fragile it all is—how many things that had always seemed engraved in monumental stone or written on parchment in permanent ink turn out to depend on flimsy traditions and disposable norms, and how much these depend on public opinion. One unfit ruler at the head of a craven party and a nihilistic rebellion by a part of the people nearly destroyed self-government, doing it great harm. Our institutions sustained a tremendous shock, but they survived.

There are other lessons. Racism is in our marrow, and enough Americans either celebrate or tolerate this evil that it came within a whisker of gaining a lasting hold on power. Like the fixation on Trump, there's a perverse temptation to dwell in glowing despair at what we've learned about the American heart of darkness, in triumphant disgust at the spectacle of a Confederate flag carried into the sacred space of the Union. Ha! See? What did you expect? *This is who we are.*

There's something pernicious about that thought. To believe that Trump showed us who we really are is no different from believing that Obama showed us who we really are. Narcissism is expressed in extremes of self-contempt as well as self-adoration. Both are paralyzing. They tell us more about the mind of the person in front of the mirror than the objective facts of the image in the glass.

America is neither a land of the free and home of the brave nor a bastion of white supremacy. Or rather, it is both, and other things as well, changing all the time and yet somehow remaining itself. Whether you see it as one or the other or something else altogether is not a neutral observation— it's a choice. Every choice satisfies a desire. Neither Sinful America nor Exceptional America, neither the 1619 Project nor the 1776 Report, tells a story that makes me want to take part. The first produces despair, the second complacency. Both are static narratives that leave no room for human agency, inspire no love to make the country better, provide no motive for getting to work. At some point you have to stop staring in the mirror and, in Langston Hughes's words, "make America again!" But that will need a better story.

We have to make changes at the largest and the most personal levels—in economic structures and in habits of thinking and acting. *We have to create the conditions of equality and acquire the art of self-government.* The two are inseparable, and doing each one makes the other possible. There are things working in our favor. We've been shocked to attention. We aren't strangers, not even in a nation of 330 million. We have our hidden code, our national creed, and our history. And we have the tools of citizenship that Greeley,

Perkins, and Rustin put to use: journalism, government, and activism. Only, they need repairing.

When Perkins turned from social work to government work, she was acknowledging that radically unequal economic conditions have to be redressed by the state. Around the same time, in 1914, Walter Lippmann wrote in his Progressive manifesto *Drift and Mastery*: "You can't expect civic virtue from a disfranchised class . . . The first item in the program of self-government is to drag the whole population well above the misery line."

A century later it's still true. What kind of civic virtue is possible for a nonunion Amazon warehouse associate putting in mandatory overtime with a fever and leaving her remote-schooled kids in the care of her elderly mother? The American passion for equality is thwarted by vastly and permanently unequal conditions. If Americans are to achieve the equality that has always attracted and always eluded us, government will have to be the prime mover, though not the only one.

Recently we've been governed by some of the worst public servants in the history of the republic, people whose names belong on a National Registry of Governance Offenders with a mandatory lifetime ban: elected representatives whose only ambition is to own their opponents on cable news; agency heads who use their power to strip public assets for private benefit; cynics, extremists, incompetent suck-ups, small-eyed crooks, and Kushners and Loefflers of all kinds.

When the new administration took office, the wreckage was everywhere. The social safety net was so shredded that millions of Americans had to go to work sick or lost health insurance during the pandemic, while state unemployment systems and public health departments nearly collapsed from malign neglect. The workplace safety administration had stopped doing the kind of inspections that were the legacy of the Triangle Shirtwaist fire, causing injuries and deaths of American workers to soar. The federal minimum wage of $7.25 is worth barely half its value fifty years ago. Antitrust enforcement leaves monopolies in place while going after smaller competitors that have to cooperate in order to survive. Labor law enforcement consistently favors corporations over unions. These conditions, largely the result of decades of anti-government ideology, turn equality into a lie, and the lie deranges everyone. The way to begin reversing the deterioration is to show the American people that government can make their lives better.

We've been ravaged by a short emergency—the pandemic and the depression-like conditions that it brought on. But the Biden administration is also facing a long emergency, which the short one has dramatized and worsened: the inequality that excludes so many Americans from full citizenship because their lives are consumed with the struggle to get through this month.

That emergency has been coming on for so long—years, decades, in some cases centuries—that you might raise an eyebrow at my use of the word. But as long as the promise of equality is mocked by the reality, and the chance of a poor kid getting into a good university is close to zero, and that chance remains the only entry point to a dignified life, then we are going to keep enduring emergencies of one kind or another. We will continue to be threatened by demagogues exploiting the people's hatred of elites. We will continue to be ruled by the incompetent and the corrupt. We will continue to tear into one another over school reopenings and vaccine distribution. Permanently unequal conditions in such a rich country are not only, in Perkins's words, "preventable" and "morally unacceptable"—they shred the social cohesion on which self-government depends. To save our democracy, we must restructure our economy to make us equal Americans.

I don't mean parity of results—Americans have never expected that. We're too hostile to the coercion it would require and have too much faith in our own efforts. Most Americans want to get rich and don't object when it happens to someone else. They object to a system in which the chance to get rich is reserved for a fixed group, raising that group to a higher status. The American consensus for equal opportunity rather than equal results is very old—Eugene Debs, the greatest American socialist, revered Lincoln, champion of the self-made man. Americans won't accept the leveling hand of government in every corner of our lives. Socialism that proclaims itself enters any election with a debilitating handicap. Having spent a decade in a socialist organization, I'm acquainted with the hairsplitting futility that these long odds impose.

An economy for equal Americans is one that gives everyone a chance not just to survive but to participate with dignity. It will take ambitious new policies. I'll lay out some of them, not because they're original or because I expect them to be achieved today, tomorrow, or ever, but because we need to know where we want to go.

The first big step is to repair the safety net so that workers and families are no longer at perpetual risk of falling through and drowning, as millions have in the pandemic. This means essentially extending the New Deal to more Americans in more areas of their lives: universal health care, child care, paid family and sick leave, stronger workplace safety protections, unemployment insurance that doesn't fail in a crisis, a living minimum wage. These are the basis for any decent life, for any American to do more than survive just below the misery line.

But shoring up the floor will not be enough. The vast lower two-thirds of the income scale, the Americans who have lost wages, jobs, and communities since the 1970s, has to be given more economic power. They need it for their own sake, as workers and citizens, and for the sake of an entire society that is lopsided in favor of business and the rich. Progressives like Lippmann and Louis Brandeis saw industrial workers as a class whose organization could check the power of the trusts and also make the immigrant masses capable of citizenship. "For only through the union can the wage-earner participate in the control of industry," Lippmann wrote, "and only through the union can he obtain the discipline needed for self-government." A cog in a machine, denied the last ounce of free agency, cannot acquire the habits and skills—negotiating, cooperating, deciding—that citizens need to realize their full potential. It was true a century ago of the Steel Trust, with its punch clocks, and it's true now of Amazon, with its scheduling algorithms.

The postindustrial workforce is weak and scattered across various sectors, most of them dominated by a few giant corporations. When Amazon opens a "fulfillment center" in a declining community, its size immediately gives it control over the local job market, allowing it to dictate wages and eliminate competition that might offer better jobs at better pay. One way to give labor more power is to make it easier to organize workers by passing labor law reform bills—the perennial campaign promises of Democratic candidates that go perennially unfulfilled. Another is to direct large-scale government investments into key national sectors—clean energy, manufacturing, education, and caregiving—to create jobs, stimulate innovation, and raise the pay and status of workers. And a third is to form new institutions for worker power that are better suited to a postindustrial economy, as Michael Lind argues in *The New Class War*: labor representation on corporate boards, collective bargaining by sector rather than company, and wage boards that set minimum terms for low-wage industries like fast food.

The oppression of the American working class is a largely untapped subject for this generation of activists. Why didn't millions of young people go into the streets in the summer of 2020 to protest against Hospital Corporation of America and Tyson Foods on behalf of nurses' aides and meat processors? There's a strain of class prejudice in Just America. "A hairdresser has to go to school for longer than you do!" a shirtless young man taunted a line of police officers during a protest in New York. "Half of you don't even have a college education, to be out here making demands about the people when you can't even read a fucking history book!" Class politics jeopardizes advantages that are harder for the educated elite to renounce than racial privilege, and the sacrifices required are more tangible. There's a moral barrier as well, since the white working class carries the mark of Trump. The cause got lost somewhere in the decades between the New Deal and critical theory. Instead, Just America embraces an ideology of rigid identity groups that keeps the professional class in its superior place, divides workers, and has little to do with the reality of an increasingly multiracial, intermarrying society. Workers of all backgrounds have much more in common than our politics acknowledges. Any viable narrative has to include them all.

Real America divides the working class in a different way. Trump's pro-worker policies always meant white Christian

Americans in the heartland and always required some other group to get hurt. The refusal of his supporters to acknowledge the pain of their fellow Americans who are Black is a great moral failure; the resentment that feeds their hostility to activist government is a costly political failure that has inflicted lasting damage on Americans of all races. But a racial reckoning directed by elites in powerful institutions is unlikely to accomplish much more than to deepen divisions, especially when it uses Just American language that stigmatizes entire groups. If anything can lower the fever of populism in Real America, which easily spikes into white nationalism, it will be this: the experience of shared responsibility in worker organizations, and improvements in people's daily lives, partly made possible by the help of a government that is manifestly on their side.

One effect of the pandemic has been to entrench the new aristocracy of Smart America. The failure of public schools to reopen sent large numbers of this generation's favored children into private schools. With a booming stock market and secure jobs, meritocrats have become rentiers who live off investments as well as incomes. The wealth that parents pass on to their children will compound and become a permanent family ticket into the upper class. Meritocrats will identify more and more with the big capitalists whom they envy and criticize, while retaining a sense of moral superiority for their achievements. As with any hereditary ruling class, political power will fall into the hands of increasingly inferior people.

One way to limit these advantages is to expand the estate tax, which was dramatically reduced by Trump and the Republican Congress. Lowering by half the level of wealth at which the tax kicks in would generate revenue on a progressive basis while still sparing families in the upper-middle class. Most important, it would force the next generation of rich children to make their way more on talent and less on blind good luck. Some scholars propose reducing the clout of professional guilds by changing licensing rules so that nurses and paralegals can do some of the work and make some of the money currently monopolized by doctors and lawyers.

The new aristocracy has to be attacked from the other side as well, by improving education for poor and middle-class children who are systematically denied a good one. Huge advantages by wealth are built into American schools at every level, and nothing is more decisive in creating permanent classes. There is no simple way to democratize education, but one radical change would be to move the funding structure of public schools away from heavy dependence on local taxes and toward federal and state taxes, so that spending on children in a rich school district like Scarsdale, New York, is no longer two or three times what it is in Arizona or Alabama. Better teachers could be attracted to poorer schools by raising pay based on hardship. In metropolitan areas, de facto school segregation—the separation of children by wealth and race into better and worse schools—can be turned around by integration plans like the ones in some New York City districts, which removed barriers to admissions based on grades.

Integration can help to equalize resources, but that won't by itself close the achievement gap. To believe that it will is magical thinking. Schools that congratulate themselves on achieving numerical diversity while they sink into intellectual mediocrity degrade the value of equality and merit. A democratic education system needs to find a way to preserve both. During the pandemic, Alison Collins, the vice president of the San Francisco Board of Education, said: "When we talk about merit, meritocracy, and especially meritocracy based on standardized testing—I'm just going to say it, in this day and age we cannot mince words—those are racist systems." But to abolish assessments, as many Just Americans want to do, and then declare that we've achieved "equity," ensures that all students receive exactly the same lousy education. Poorer children stand a chance only if they receive rigorous teaching and tutoring, and academic standards are set high for everyone.

In 1964, Bayard Rustin helped organize a one-day boycott of New York's public schools to protest de facto segregation. Almost half a million children stayed home—the largest single civil rights protest in American history. But when activists in the late sixties began calling for separate courses for Black college students, Rustin strongly objected to an education "that cannot really prepare them for the kind of life they have to live . . . I shall continue to advocate those means by which Negroes can obtain the educational skills, as well as the political and economic power, that will enable them to achieve equality *within* the context of American society." Likewise, the current drive to "dismantle" the classics for their "white supremacy" and "disrupt" Shakespeare for "centering white male voices" deprives all students of the intellectual and moral benefits of that vital, vanishing thing—a humanistic education. It makes students easy marks for the shallow dogmas of both social justice and consumer capitalism. It puts a truly democratic education out of their reach. Equal American schools would be well funded, integrated, and committed to teaching Shakespeare *and* August Wilson to all students.

Realizing these ideas will take a long hard slog of many years against the headwinds of resistance from opposition forces and around the structural obstacles embedded in the Constitution. The important thing is for the country to start moving in this direction—for Americans to see the beginning of change. Most of these ideas will enjoy wide support, especially from working-class voters of all races. They don't have to reach the heavenly shores of brotherhood and sisterhood—just a modicum of trust. The benefits will accrue not only to this or that group, but to the whole society. Weakening the new aristocracy and restoring the dignity of labor will help to break up the concentrated power that corrupts our politics and puts all of the economy's rewards in the hands of speculators and meritocrats. It will make inequality of smarts less decisive in sorting out our fates. It will bring other values back to American life. It will allow Americans to look at one another as equals.

At the top of our economy, invisible monopolies reach down and wrap us within their smothering embrace in everything we do. Every sector, from food and gas to money and information, is controlled by just a few giant companies, in some cases by just one. Their presence is so dominating that we hardly notice them.

Monopolies threaten equality in ways large and small. They capture legislatures and crush the voices of ordinary citizens. They buy or kill off smaller competition, stifling the creative drive of future entrepreneurs. They seduce consumers with low prices and automated convenience, and in return those consumers surrender their privacy and, in some ways, their free will; if price or quality takes a turn for the worse, consumers have nowhere to go. Monopolies degrade communities by destroying Main Street businesses and drawing away wealth from depressed regions to a few thriving megalopolises. In the new gig economy, industry concentration in two or three winning hands forces workers to remain contractors, denying them the barest protections such as health insurance.

And yet the whole system depends on our acquiescence. If a ride-share app is quick and easy, if one-click shopping beats driving to the mall, if a too-big-to-fail bank has branches all over the city, it's hard to see all the negative consequences of monopoly, or want to do much about them. So in 2020 voters in California, who gave Biden 5 million more votes than Trump, also passed a referendum to overturn a new state law that would have allowed drivers for Uber and Lyft the status and rights of employees. As long as prices stay low and services efficient, who really wants change? Even if you feel a vague objection now and then, you still have to live in the world of the behemoths.

The Progressives of Perkins's era attacked the trusts not simply because they were big, but because they threatened the freedom of the independent owner, the industrial worker, and the citizen. In 1912 Louis Brandeis told a congressional hearing, "We cannot maintain democratic conditions in America if we allow organizations to arise in our midst with the power of the Steel Corporation." He called it "the curse of bigness"—the threat from concentrated power to individual character, to the capacities we need to govern ourselves. The answer was to break up monopolies and give workers the chance to develop the art of self-government in their own organizations. "Our objective is the making of men and women who shall be free—self-respecting members of a democracy—and who shall be worthy of respect," Brandeis wrote. "But democracy in any sphere is a serious undertaking. It substitutes self-restraint for external restraint."

The democratic fear of monopoly remained central to American politics until the Reagan era. Then a new idea arose from the narrative of Free America. As long as concentrated economic power brings efficiency and lower prices, the idea went, the government has no business breaking it up. The measure of monopoly should be the consumer, not the citizen—the market, not democracy. This has been the U.S. government's antitrust policy ever since Reagan. The result is all around us.

Forty years ago, the narrative of Free America located its enemy in the high taxes, onerous regulations, and over-weening bureaucrats of big government. The narrative mechanically repeats the same mantra to this day—listen to the speeches of Republicans in Congress or the policies of pro-business think tanks and lobbies. But the facts have long since changed—many of them refute the mantra—and the narrative needs to change with them. Today the greatest obstacle to economic freedom is monopoly power. By allowing corporations to dominate both government and workers, Free America has weakened the countervailing powers that are as necessary to genuinely free markets as checks and balances are to free governments.

In recent years a new anti-monopoly movement has emerged, partly inspired by the Progressives, with new ideas for the old desire to make all citizens capable of participating in our political and economic life. Its most famous advocate is Senator Elizabeth Warren, who often echoes Brandeis, and who told the story of Frances Perkins one night in a campaign speech in Washington Square, a block from the Triangle Shirtwaist building. A second antitrust age would increase innovation, decentralize power, revitalize depressed regions, and free both workers and small businesses to compete. Its strongest supporters should be Free Americans.

C reating the conditions of equality requires new structures and policies. Acquiring the art of self-government needs something else—new ways of thinking and living.

"The real trouble with us professors was that we were absorbed in our day-to-day tasks," Marc Bloch confessed in *Strange Defeat* after the fall of France. "Most of us can say with some justice that we were good workmen. Is it equally true to say that we were good citizens?" My trade is journalism—one of the main tools for self-government—and I have to ask myself the same question.

In some ways the media, along with politics, is returning to the Civil War era. The twentieth-century idea of the press as an independent authority, rising above narrow political views in pursuit of "objectivity," has been in decline and disfavor in the twenty-first. Objectivity is always an aspiration more than a reality. It's like an internal brake on the normal human tendency toward bias—a restraining ideal in a healthy democracy. But media organizations of all kinds have been sucked into the vortex of polarization, and in many cases they do all they can to further it. They're under pressures that are political, financial, and technological, all pushing media to be faster, louder, simpler, and more partisan.

Barack Obama recently described the kind of coverage he once received as a state politician in Illinois. "Even as late as 2008, typically when I went into a small town, there's a small-town newspaper, and the owner or editor is a conservative guy with a crew cut, maybe, and a bow tie, and he's been a Republican for years," Obama recalled. "He doesn't have a lot of patience for tax-and-spend liberals, but he'll take a meeting with me, and he'll write an editorial that says, 'He's a liberal Chicago lawyer, but he seems like a decent enough guy, had some good ideas'; and the local TV station will cover me straight." Now, Obama added, the paper is gone, and every television in town is showing conservative news.

"Even as late as 2008." That was the year I began to notice a change. During the campaign, Tom Giffey, an editor of the Eau Claire, Wisconsin, *Leader-Telegram*—one of the few remaining sources of local news in his region—told me that he no longer received real letters to the editor, just cut-and-paste emails. "In the old days, there were Republican or Democratic newspapers, but there was more of a level playing field and both sides had to argue from the same set of facts," Giffey said. "Now we're in an age where you can simply reinforce your own viewpoints. And it's hard to have a discussion of the facts when you're dealing with two separate sets of facts—two sets of talking points that came down from on high. With the Internet, all of us were going to be content producers, but it's become an echo chamber."

A couple of months before the election, residents of a small town in Ohio were discussing the race with me over breakfast, and they used just the same words as cable news talking heads—throwing out terms like "convention bounce" and "executive experience." I asked about local issues, but they wanted only to talk about the national politics that people in Washington and California discussed, and in the same language. This had become more real to them than anything in the lives they were living in southeastern Ohio. "Partisanship has crept into every crease in this country," a building contractor named Dave Herbert said.

These things—nationalization of all politics and news, partisanship in forgotten places, polarization of facts in the Internet echo chamber—were revelations to me in 2008. Since then the trends have all grown more intense. Even the respectable media can't escape them. We still get echoes of the old objectivity in the impersonal language of news stories, but it's like a traditional religious practice that continues after most of the faithful have stopped believing. Over the past decade, especially the past five years or so, leading news outlets have moved toward one partisan corner or another just to survive. We don't expect anything else from cable news, but it's also true of organizations like *The New York Times*, *The Washington Post*, and National Public Radio. Compare a story from ten years ago—political bias is strikingly more evident today, even on subjects tangential to politics, such as education or theater.

After Trump's election victory in 2016, the *Times* issued a mea culpa for failing to understand and prepare its readers for the result. The paper sent reporters out to the heartland, almost as if it were opening a foreign bureau, to interview Trump voters. One reporter profiled an Ohio welder who owned four cats, loved *Seinfeld*, and had joined a neo-Nazi group. The paper was thoroughly savaged by readers and other journalists for "normalizing hate." That put an end to the *Times*'s experiment. In 2020 its coverage of Trump's world was even more constrained than in 2016. Readers had to wait until after the election to receive the shocking news that Trump's support among Black, Latino, and immigrant men had gone up, and that the only identity group whose support for Trump had declined was white men.

The push to change didn't come from the top of the media. It emerged from below, among younger reporters and read- ers. Some of the most decorated journalism of the past few years has rejected "objectivity" in pursuit of a different ideal: "moral clarity." What would it even mean to be objective about Trump, or racism? There is no "on the other hand"! The correct tone is Greeley's in his pre–Civil War *Tribune*: "If the slavery propagandists are ready for the inevitable struggle, let no retreat be beaten by the champions of universal Free- dom. The people are looking on." But most stories don't submit to our desire for certainty. When they appear to, it might just mean that we've crushed them flat. The problem with moral clarity is how much of life and news gets lost in its glare. It overpowers subjects more than it illuminates them. Writers stop seeing the little flaws and contradictions of actual life, and stop wanting to—they and their readers have only to bask in the warmth of a blinding glow. Moral clarity also induces fear, like an interrogation light.

There's an important difference between our anxious,

wrathful twenty-first-century media and that of the confident nineteenth. The anti-slavery press, like Greeley's *Tribune*, was every bit as partisan as *Vox* or *Breitbart*, but it believed that free expression and dissenting views would serve the cause of justice. It didn't try to shut down the self-justifications of the Slave Power; it believed that they would discredit themselves. Today, hostility to free expression has taken root in a new generation of journalists. Lacking the power to censor, some use the power to shame, intimidate, and ostracize, even turning it on their colleagues. But in essence they are asking for their own destruction.

In an atmosphere of stifling conformism—a desire for the crowd's affirmation or a fear of the sound of your own voice—honest, clear, original work is not going to flourish, and without it, the politicians and tech moguls and TV demagogues have less to worry about. Fear breeds self-censorship, and self-censorship is more insidious than the state-imposed kind, because it's a surer way of killing the impulse to think, which requires an unfettered mind. A writer can still write while hiding from the thought police. But a writer who carries the thought police around in his head, who always feels compelled to ask: *Can I say this? Do I have a right? Is my terminology correct? Will my allies get angry? Will it help my enemies? Will it get me ratioed on Twitter?*—that writer's work will soon become lifeless. Any writer who is afraid to tell people what they don't want to hear has chosen the wrong profession.

The first step to renewing a democratic press is for its

owners, practitioners, and readers to find the moral courage to think for themselves and stand on their own if necessary, even if the cost is high. But the changes also have to be structural, because technology and finance have driven the media into an economy of scarcity amid plenty.

The transformation of the information economy and the effect on our minds are so radical that we're whipsawed almost minute to minute by immense changes without understanding their meaning. From its beginning, Silicon Valley combined the narrative of Free America (no regulation) with that of Smart America (meritocracy with an idealistic global mission). Facebook, Google, Amazon, and Apple grow as if they are part of the natural order of things, our air and water, our very minds, while they swallow competitors and invade every private corner of our lives by offering their services for little or nothing. At the start of the century the tech giants blasted the financial basis of journalism to pieces by seizing its content and giving it away—and publishers were shortsighted enough to scramble over this cliff voluntarily. Then tech monopolies devoured the vast share of the industry's advertising, targeting users with all the personal information they had naïvely turned over. Newspapers began to wither away or disappear altogether. In the first two decades of the century, consolidation and closures have eliminated more than two thousand local papers in America and half the jobs in journalism, leaving behind an army of highly skilled, unemployed workers and a misinformed, disengaged public.

Technology companies drove the survivors into a mindset

of engineered efficiency—the belief that data tells you everything of value. "Just like the tech companies, journalism has
come to fetishize data. And this data has come to corrupt
journalism," Franklin Foer writes in *World Without Mind*.
"Once journalists come to know what works, which stories
yield traffic, they will pursue what works. This is the definition of pandering and it has horrific consequences." The
quest for clicks heavily influences what and how journalists
write, while algorithmic news feeds pull readers into spaces
where they congregate with the like-minded in shared hatred
for those outside. Everyone has a voice, but everyone uses it
to conform, and the consensus becomes more extreme as
it hardens like plaque.

The Internet was supposed to replace the discredited gatekeepers of old media with freedom and equality for everyone. Instead we have half a dozen new gatekeepers, the most
powerful monopolists in the world, and we are less equal than
before. Large regions of the country have gone dark, enclos-
ing citizens in private worlds of simplifications and lies. The
handful of surviving news organizations so dominate the
space that they've turned into hothouses of petty intrigue.
Journalists inhabit incestuous circles of backscratching and
backbiting, with dwindling incentives to do the unglamor-
ous work of digging up corruption and finding out how other
Americans live. The infinitude of the Internet has created
such fierce competition for diminishing jobs and attention
spans that journalists pour large amounts of unpaid time and
effort into sucking up, piling on, and showing off on social

media in the endless pursuit of followers and likes. The psychological difference between certain blue-check Twitter accounts and the invaders livestreaming selfies as they strolled through the Capitol rotunda is smaller than it seems. The masters of technology make anxious narcissists of us all.

The media can free itself from the forces that arouse its self-destructive impulses. Some of the tools are already in our hands—antitrust laws to break up tech monopolies. Other tools would change the structure of the game—for example, regulations to classify digital platforms as publishers, with the resulting responsibilities and liabilities. Tech critics have proposed legislation to ban personalized ads, which would send some advertising back to news organizations and perhaps contribute to a revival of local and regional news. Some tools will have to be invented—new ways to support local journalism, new structures for social media that diminish the power of profit and make the Internet a more truly civic space.

Many journalists without brand names on marquee platforms are doing superb investigative and other reporting, using digital technology to gather data, reach a far-flung audience, and illuminate injustices, as Greeley's *Tribune* used the telegraph and the steam-powered rotary press to tell workers in New York what slavers were doing in Kansas. Many readers still crave this kind of painstaking work, appreciate it when they encounter it, and are willing to pay for it if they're asked to. The demand could produce a flowering of new outlets that will attract talented newcomers as well as refugees from established media as it increasingly loses its way.

We need journalists who are rewarded when they refrain from scratching their Twitter itch and discover their fellow Americans. We need journalism that is independent and imaginative enough to go to places that Mark Zuckerberg never sees. We need citizens who can listen to one another while thinking for themselves. And we need to affirm the value of free expression for any of this to matter.

Our idea of activism has come down to the act of protest. It's an indispensable civic tool for dramatizing a cause, heightening social tensions, and claiming the attention of those in power. But beginning with the Tea Party, we've had a decade of continuous protest in both Real and Just America—proof of a breakdown in institutional politics. We need a new form of activism in the coming decade, the kind that Rustin was reaching for in the years after the great civil rights victories. We need an activism of cohesion. We need an activism that doesn't separate Americans into like-minded factions but brings Americans together across tribal lines.

"Nothing is more wonderful than the art of being free," Tocqueville wrote, "but nothing is harder to learn how to use than freedom." To acquire the art of self-government, he believed, citizens have to be together. They have to come out of the isolation of their individualism and experience government at a level local enough that it brings them face-to-face. He congratulated the founders on building a structure in which government had to function not just in distant capitals but also in towns and villages. Tocqueville also believed that the civic associations he saw proliferating in nineteenth-century America, forms of self-help that substituted for the powerful aristocrats of European societies, performed a similar role to town meetings: "Feelings and ideas are renewed, the heart enlarged, and the understanding developed only by the reciprocal action of men one upon another."

In the age of toxic polarization and digital information monopoly, everything conspires to defeat the art of self-government. Civic clubs and newspapers are disappearing from our towns. The state is remote and indifferent—most Americans encounter it as a check in the mail, a tax form, a jury summons, and a ballot. The last is the only experience that comes close to enlarging the heart. As for town meetings, they attract the loudest among us, and most normal citizens avoid them. The more political power is concentrated in a few hands, the less government at the local level means anything.

Historically, the federal government has been the guarantor of individual freedom and equality, which states and localities are likely to take away. But in the Trump years liberals began to realize that small can be beautiful, and that power at the local level, as long as it doesn't abridge individual rights, can get more done for the public good and *show it being done* than divided Washington, where reform legislation always faces long odds. In the 2020 election, local officials who had to face their neighbors and constituents prevented the opportunists of our national politics from disenfranchising the entire country. The example of the New Deal, which created giant bureaucracies and an imperial presidency, doesn't hold all the answers and even contains some of the problems.

As town meetings and civic groups disappear, we've tried to practice self-government on the Internet. In its early days there were utopian hopes for the electronic town hall. Gavin Newsom, the governor of California, wrote a book about how digital technology would make government more efficient and inclusive, restoring its connection to the governed. But the masters of big tech knew that the best way to keep us online was to feed our appetites, our tribal identities, our vanity, our rage. It's a lot easier to flame or dunk on someone whose face isn't right in front of you. And the pandemic has made us profoundly unreal to one another. It's driven many Americans into varieties of digital insanity.

The most obvious way to give Americans the power to act as self-governing citizens is to make their voices meaningful. A new democracy law should prohibit state legislatures from raising barriers that disenfranchise voters, most often Black Americans; end the partisan gerrymandering by which politicians lock in permanent advantages; and use public funding to increase the power of small campaign donations and reduce the legal corruption brought on by the Supreme Court's *Citizens United* decision. Such a law should make voting more accessible through automatic registration, but also make it mandatory, like jury duty, with fines for the tens of millions of eligible voters who neglect to exercise the franchise.

Measures like these—long shots in our present politics—would not end bitter divisions, nor should they. Instead, they would bring the governed closer to government by taking power away from an undemocratic system and putting it in the hands of ordinary people.

But self-government starts in ourselves. The most basic way Americans can acquire what Tocqueville called "habits of the heart" is by killing their Twitter or Facebook accounts and spending time in the physical presence of other Americans who don't look or talk or think like them. Study after study shows that antagonistic groups begin to lose their mutual hostility and acquire trust when they have to work together, as long as they're engaged in a specific project, with outside help. The best idea for making America again as a single country might be to require a year of national service, in military or civilian form, repaid by scholarship, training stipend, or small-business grant.

Just as Israelis and Palestinians, Bosnian Serbs and Muslims, Northern Irish Protestants and Catholics are brought together to build a school or perform a play and lower the murderous temperature in their countries, Americans from red and blue areas can come together in common endeavors. They might find out that the other is less a threat to the republic than they supposed. At least they will be in the company of actual human beings.

One of the January 6 rioters was a fifty-eight-year-old handyman and loner from rural Virginia named Doug Sweet. When he was thirteen, he visited the Capitol for the first time, and he breathed the spirit of equality: "I have a right to be here. This is America's building. My voice counts as good as anyone else's here." Forty-five years later, he entered the Capitol for the second time, now as an invader with a head full of conspiracy theories. Between 1975 and 2021 whatever tied Doug Sweet to democracy and reason snapped. In his delusion he was convinced that his voice was no longer as good as anyone else's—it had been stolen from him, and he had every right to barge in and take away the voices of 81 million other Americans in order to get his own back.

What do we do about Doug Sweet? Punish him for his actions. Keep an eye on him. Anticipate more violence and prevent it with tools the state already has. Expose, isolate, and discredit his views as much as possible so that the spread slows and is largely confined to the sphere of private fantasy. Drive his champions out of public office. Never let the American people forget what he did.

And then? What about the millions of sympathizers? We can't jail them all, or deport them, or destroy them in total war and then rebuild their communities while reeducating their children in democratic values. I'm tempted to say the hell with them, ignore them as long as they don't break the law. Let's make America again without them.

But we can't ignore them—they won't let us. So we have to look for those ideas and policies and dreams that will make it possible to live together as equal Americans.

When I began this book, millions of voters were standing in long lines and there was not yet a vaccine. As I finish it, Trump is gone and people are lining up for shots. He left us less free, less equal, more divided, more delusional, more alone, deeper in debt, swampier, dirtier, meaner, sicker, and deader. But he's gone, and we're still here.

The early days of 2021 carried a distinct flavor of 1861. President Joe Biden and Vice President Kamala Harris were inaugurated under heavy guard, in a ceremony closed to the public for security reasons. Twenty-five thousand troops were garrisoned in the Capitol to prevent insurrection by seditionists. Elected representatives tried to bring guns into Congress. Members of the House almost came to blows and no longer felt safe in one another's presence. We know who the Confederates and Unionists are in our simmering conflict. "One of them would make war rather than let the nation survive," Lincoln said in his Second Inaugural, recalling the circumstances of his first, "and the other would accept war rather than let it perish."

Two mornings after the assault on the Capitol, I woke up with benign paroxysmal positional vertigo, a disorder of the crystals in the inner ear. With every step, my point-of-view camera jostled. The stairs below me scoped downward to a fifty-foot drop. I tired easily as I walked a long dark hallway at the end of which was a tiny point of light that never got bigger. All of this made perfect sense.

I wonder if I've lost a basic knack for human association. We orient ourselves by other people, and it seems I've grown dizzy without them. I can no longer imagine the time of separation ever ending, but in fact it's almost over. We're getting ready to return to life. When we can finally show our faces, will we know one another? Will we dare to embrace? What will be left of the ties between us? Will we want to be together?

In a dark hour at the end of the sixties, an education official in Cleveland asked Bayard Rustin to write a letter for an exhibit that was intended to explain to city schoolchildren "the magnificent times in which we live." It was 1969. Cleveland was suffering from riots, the loss of industrial jobs, Black anger, and white flight. That year the Cuyahoga River grew so polluted that it caught fire, the famous amusement park on Lake Erie closed forever, and downtown Cleveland was emptying out. The city was in deep trouble, from which, half a century later, it still hasn't recovered.

Rustin sat down and wrote:

Dear Children of Cleveland:

There are two concepts, each of which is drawn from the noblest part of our American heritage, which explain the nature of the aspirations of the poor and oppressed people in this country and throughout the world. These concepts are democracy and equality.

Democracy means the right to participate in determining the political destiny of one's community, city, state, and nation.

After describing self-government, Rustin went on: "If, then, democracy is political, equality is economic and social." Equality means the right to a life without poverty and its many ills, without discrimination—the opportunity for all people "to realize their full potential and dignity as human beings." He ended the letter by saying that, in the pursuit of these things, the means have to be the same as the ends: "We must remember that we cannot hope to achieve democracy and equality in such a way that would destroy the very kind of society we hope to build."

Rustin didn't assure the children that their country had already reached this promised land, or warn them that it could never get there. Democracy is a continuing experiment with no end point of perfection, no eternal truths outside human action. Those truths that we hold to be self-evident, the ones that Rustin explained to the children of Cleveland, will survive only if we can realize them through our own efforts. Self-government puts all the responsibility in our hands. No strongman or expert or privileged class or algorithm can do it for us. As soon as we abandon the task, the common skeleton unknits and collapses in a heap of bones.

All of this asks us to place more faith in ourselves and one another than we can bear. On some days the project seems preposterous and the effort exhausting. But I am an American and there's no escape. We've never known any other way of life. We have to make this one.

FURTHER READING

Last Best Hope was inspired by political pamphlets from other periods of crisis: *Democratic Vistas*, by Walt Whitman (1868); *Drift and Mastery: An Attempt to Diagnose the Current Unrest*, by Walter Lippmann (1914); *Strange Defeat: A Statement of Evidence Written in 1940*, by Marc Bloch (1940); *The Lion and the Unicorn: Socialism and the English Genius*, by George Orwell (1941); and *The Fire Next Time*, by James Baldwin (1963).

Alexis de Tocqueville's *Democracy in America* (1840) gave me fundamental insights and remains the most profound book I know on the subject. Two essays by Bryan Garsten guided my thinking on equality and self-government: "Will Tocqueville's Dilemma Crash America?" (*Tablet*, April 16, 2019) and "How to Protect America from the Next Donald Trump" (*New York Times*, November 9, 2020). I also benefited from classic works of scholarship: *Anti-Intellectualism in American Life*, by Richard Hofstadter (Vintage, 1963); *The Impending Crisis: America Before the Civil War, 1848–1861*, by David M. Potter (Harper Perennial, 2011); *Achieving Our Country: Leftist Thought in Twentieth-Century America*, by Richard Rorty (Harvard University Press, 1998); and *John Dewey and American Democracy*, by Robert B. West-brook (Cornell University Press, 1991).

In "Four Americas" I was helped by *The Conservative Intellectual Movement in America Since 1945*, by George H. Nash (ISI Books, 2008); *The Meritocracy Trap: How America's Foundational Myth Feeds Inequality, Dismantles the Middle Class, and Devours the Elite*, by Daniel Markovits (Penguin Press, 2019); "The Way Out of America's Zero-Sum Thinking on Race and Wealth," by Heather C. McGhee (*The New York Times*, February 13, 2021); *The Tyranny of Merit: What's Become of the Common Good?*, by Michael J. Sandel (Farrar, Straus and Giroux, 2020); *Who Are We? The Challenges to America's National Identity*, by Samuel P. Huntington (Simon and Schuster, 2005); and "How 'Elite Overproduction' and 'Lawyer Glut' Could Ruin the U.S.," by Peter Turchin (*Bloomberg View*, November 14, 2016).

In "Equal America" I was inspired by essays in *Nobody Knows My Name*, by James Baldwin (Dell, 1964); *Shadow and Act*, by Ralph Ellison (Vintage, 1995); and *The Omni-Americans: Some Alternatives to the Folklore of White Supremacy*, by Albert Murray (Library of America, 2020). My ideas were shaped and challenged by interviews on *The Ezra Klein Show* podcast and by *Divided We Fall: America's Secession Threat and How to Restore Our Nation*, by David French (St. Martin's Press, 2020).

In "Equalizers," the sketch of Horace Greeley drew on *Abraham Lincoln and Horace Greeley*, by Gregory A. Borchard (Southern Illinois University Press, 2019); *Lincoln*, by David Herbert Donald (Simon and Schuster, 1995); *The Field of Blood: Violence in Congress and the Road to Civil War*, by Joanne B. Freeman (Farrar, Straus and Giroux, 2018); *Recollections of a Busy Life*, by Horace Greeley (J. B. Ford & Co., 1868); *What Hath God Wrought? The Transformation of America, 1815–1848*, by Daniel Walker Howe (Oxford University Press, 2007); and *Horace Greeley: Champion of American Freedom*, by Robert C. Williams (New York University Press, 2006). I wrote about Frances Perkins with the help of *The Woman Behind the New Deal: The Life and Legacy of Frances Perkins—Social Security, Unemployment Insurance, and the Minimum Wage*, by Kristin Downey (Anchor Books, 2010); *The Roosevelt I Knew*, by Frances Perkins (Penguin Classics, 2011); and *The Republic for Which It Stands: The United States During Reconstruction and the Gilded Age, 1865–1896*, by Richard White (Oxford University Press, 2017). For the sketch of Bayard Rustin, I am grateful for the two collections of his writings, *I Must Resist: Bayard Rustin's Life in Letters*, ed. Michael G. Long (City Lights Books, 2012), and *Time on Two Crosses: The Collective Writings of Bayard Rustin*, ed. Devon W. Carbado and Donald Weise (University of Chicago Press, 2003); and for his biography, *Lost Prophet: The Life and Times of Bayard Rustin*, by John D'Emilio (Cleis Press, 2015).

In "Make America Again" I learned a lot about monopoly,

technology, and class in contemporary America from *Monopolized: Life in the Age of Corporate Power*, by David Dayen (New Press, 2020); *World Without Mind: The Existential Threat of Big Tech*, by Franklin Foer (Penguin, 2018); *The New Class War: Saving Democracy from the Managerial Elite*, by Michael Lind (Portfolio/Penguin, 2020); *Liberty from All Masters: The New American Autocracy vs. the Will of the People*, by Barry C. Lynn (St. Martin's Press, 2020); *Fulfillment: Winning and Losing in One-Click America*, by Alec MacGillis (Farrar, Straus and Giroux, 2021); *Goliath: The 100-Year War Between Monopoly Power and Democracy*, by Matt Stoller (Simon and Schuster, 2020); and "What Happened to Social Mobility in America?," by Branko Milanovic (*Foreign Affairs*, January 8, 2021). Some ideas for democratic renewal draw on *Our Common Purpose: Reinventing American Democracy for the 21st Century*, a project of the American Academy of Arts and Sciences, co-chaired by Danielle Allen, Stephen B. Heintz, and Eric P. Liu. The story of Doug Sweet is told in "One Trump Fan's Descent into the U.S. Capitol Mob," by Michael M. Phillips, Jennifer Levitz, and Jim Oberman (*Wall Street Journal*, January 10, 2021).

ACKNOWLEDGMENTS

This book was conceived and written during the pandemic of 2020–21. I'm thankful to friends who provided essential companionship during the long separation: David Becker, Tom Casciato, Rinne Groff, Kathy Hughes, Amy Waldman, and Georgia West.

To friends who read the manuscript and provided ideas, criticism, and encouragement: Daniel Bergner, Dexter Filkins, Frank Foer, Bryan Garsten, Samantha Hill, Mark Lilla, Alec MacGillis, and Thomas Williams. And to Christian Kerr for valuable and timely research.

To friends and colleagues at *The Atlantic* who gave me a wonderful new home: Yoni Appelbaum, David Bradley, Jeff Goldberg, Ann Hulbert, Laurene Powell Jobs, Adrienne LaFrance, Don Peck, Yvonne Rolzhausen, Scott Stossel, and Denise Wills.

To Sarah Chalfant at the Wylie Agency for her enduring support, and her belief in a project that wasn't self-evident to me.

ACKNOWLEDGMENTS

To friends and colleagues at Farrar, Straus and Giroux and Jonathan Cape for welcoming me back: Mitzi Angel, Eric Chinski, Jonathan Galassi, Michal Shavit, and this book's brilliant editor, Alex Star.

To you, Laura: *Last Best Hope* and its author owe you everything, so there's nothing to say. And to the pandemic, for one thing only: the amount of time I got to spend with Laura, Charlie, Julia, and Neptune.

A NOTE ABOUT THE AUTHOR

George Packer is a staff writer at *The Atlantic* and the author of many previous books of nonfiction, including *The Unwinding* (winner of the National Book Award), *The Assassins' Gate* (winner of the New York Public Library's Helen Bernstein Book Award for Excellence in Journalism and the Overseas Press Club's Cornelius Ryan Award), and *Our Man* (finalist for the Pulitzer Prize and winner of the Hitchens Prize and the Los Angeles Times Book Prize for biography). He is also the author of two novels and a play, *Betrayed* (winner of the Lucille Lortel Award for Outstanding Off-Broadway Play), and is the editor of a two-volume edition of the essays of George Orwell.